ELEVATE

ELEVATE

Shannah Kennedy
Colleen Callander

PENGUIN LIFE

AN IMPRINT OF

PENGUIN BOOKS

PENGUIN LIFE

UK | USA | Canada | Ireland | Australia
India | New Zealand | South Africa | China

Penguin Life is part of the Penguin Random House group of companies whose addresses can be found at global.penguinrandomhouse.com

Penguin
Random House
Australia

First published by Penguin Life in 2023

While the utmost care has been taken in researching and compiling *Elevate*, the information contained in this book is not intended as a substitute for professional medical advice. You should obtain professional advice from a medical practitioner before making lifestyle changes relating to your health.

Cover design by Adam Laszczuk © Penguin Random House Australia Pty Ltd
Infographics by Rebecca King © Penguin Random House Australia Pty Ltd
Author photograph by Susan Bradfield
Internal design by Post Pre-press, Australia
Typeset in 12/17 pt Bembo MT Pro by Post Pre-press, Australia

Printed and bound in Australia by Griffin Press, an accredited
ISO AS/NZS 14001 Environmental Management Systems printer

 A catalogue record for this
book is available from the
NATIONAL LIBRARY OF AUSTRALIA   National Library of Australia

ISBN 978 1 76134 111 3

penguin.com.au

MIX
Paper | Supporting
responsible forestry
FSC® C018684

We at Penguin Random House Australia acknowledge that Aboriginal and Torres Strait Islander peoples are the Traditional Custodians and the first storytellers of the lands on which we live and work. We honour Aboriginal and Torres Strait Islander peoples' continuous connection to Country, waters, skies and communities. We celebrate Aboriginal and Torres Strait Islander stories, traditions and living cultures; and we pay our respects to Elders past and present.

To all the remarkable individuals who have been instrumental in our lives and in the creation of this collaborative work. It is through your unwavering support, guidance and expertise that this book, designed to help you take your life from ordinary to extraordinary, has come to life.

Contents

Introduction

Unlock the Extraordinary Within

As a person, I'm just trying to be better than I was yesterday and continue to elevate

GABRIELLA WILSON

You have one precious life. Every day, life is being lived, consciously or unconsciously, right here, right now! The big question is: do you want to live a life of ordinary or extraordinary?

In our careers as CEO and coach over the last two decades, we have met so many people who spend a lot of time thinking or talking about what they want in life but very few who have the clarity, focus or plan to take substantial steps towards realising their goals and embracing a life of purpose and passion. We want to change that and help you become one of those few who can truly transform your life and elevate from ordinary to extraordinary.

About Us

Shannah has forged an enviable career as an author and life strategist and has coached elite athletes, CEOs, entrepreneurs, sporting leaders and high-performing executives and teams. Her proven expertise enables clients to gain control of their lives to achieve their visions and goals.

Colleen spent thirteen years as the CEO of two of Australia's iconic fashion brands: Sportsgirl and Sussan. She has a wealth of knowledge and a proven track record in building brands, establishing winning cultures and creating environments that allow people to be inspired and empowered throughout her thirty-year retail career.

Together, as women in our fifties, we have personally experienced the real struggle of balancing a successful career, raising a family and maintaining optimal health and fitness. We fully understand the challenges that come with juggling professional and personal responsibilities.

But we also understand the importance of investing in a long-term life plan, putting aside time to gain clarity of thought and taking action to kick-start change. We have seen how this high-performance approach can elevate life and leadership to new heights.

Unlock the Extraordinary Within

In this book we invite you to embark on a transformative journey of human elevation, unlocking the profound potential that lies within you and guiding you to tap into it to create a life of incredible health, success, happiness and fulfilment.

Our approach centres around the concept of human elevation and the pursuit of greatness in three pillars:

Pillar 1: Life: Embracing ownership and empowerment in your journey
Pillar 2: Leadership: Embracing the power of influence to lead with purpose
Pillar 3: Longevity: Embracing the foundation of health and a feeling of fulfilment as the keys to lasting success in life

The first pillar we will explore is 'Life', which serves as the foundation for the other pillars of leadership and longevity. Within this section, we will delve into personal growth and self-improvement, empowering you to take ownership of your journey and embrace your true potential. Discover how:

▲ By identifying and harnessing your unique strengths, you can use them to enhance your life and achieve your goals.

▲ Your values shape your decisions and actions, providing purpose and authenticity for a fulfilling life.

▲ Creating a clear vision, defining your goals and outlining the necessary steps will set the direction for your life's journey.

▲ Transforming your mindset is vital for personal growth and success.

▲ Your health plays a fundamental role in a fulfilling life.

▲ Elevating your confidence and overcoming self-doubt will help you believe in yourself and pursue your dreams with resilience.

By embracing ownership and empowerment through these transformative steps, you will lay a solid foundation for a life of growth, success, happiness and fulfilment. This first pillar sets the stage for your personal development, enabling you to thrive in the subsequent pillars of leadership and longevity.

The second pillar we will explore is 'Leadership', which focuses on embracing the power of influence and leading with purpose. Within this section, we will delve into various aspects of leadership to empower you to make a positive impact and inspire others.

Discover how:

▲ Your words, actions and presence allow you to positively shape the way you lead, both personally and professionally.

▲ To define and authentically communicate your personal brand to build trust and credibility as a leader.

▲ You can foster a growth-orientated, collaborative and innovative culture.

▲ Kindness strengthens relationships, builds trust and inspires loyalty.

▲ Setting high-performance goals aligned with your vision and values will keep you motivated and focused to achieve your objectives.

▲ To create positive habits that support your goals.

This second pillar sets the stage for you to become an influential and purpose-driven leader, making a positive impact in all aspects of your life.

The third pillar we will explore is 'Longevity', which emphasises the importance of fulfilment for lasting success. Within this section, we will delve into various aspects of living a fulfilling life, empowering you to prioritise your well-being and create a sustainable future. Discover how:

▲ To recognise the signs of burnout, maintain a healthy work–life balance and manage stress.

▲ By prioritising self-care and setting boundaries, you can avoid burnout and sustain your energy and motivation.

▲ Mastering high-performance planning can optimise your time and productivity, so you can achieve your goals while maintaining balance and well-being.

▲ By identifying activities and relationships that contribute to your happiness, you can enhance overall life satisfaction.

▲ By pursuing meaningful endeavours and connecting with others, you can experience a profound sense of fulfilment.

▲ Prioritising self-care allows you to replenish your energy and reduce stress.

▲ Recognising and celebrating your progress reinforces motivation and self-belief.

This third pillar empowers you to prioritise well-being and ensure lasting success.

Together, these three pillars are all you need for a balanced and outstanding life.

This book is about transcending the limitations that hold us back and unleashing the extraordinary potential that resides within each of us. It is about elevating our thoughts, beliefs and actions to create a life that is truly remarkable.

We share insights and strategies drawn from our own experiences as a CEO and coach, providing you with a proven system and practical techniques for personal and professional success. We believe that by elevating ourselves, we can also elevate the lives of those around us, becoming catalysts for positive change in our families, communities and organisations.

Elevating your life is a continuous process of growth and self-discovery. It requires dedication, commitment and a willingness to step outside of your comfort zone. We provide you with the tools and techniques to create your own action plan – a roadmap to help you craft your own extraordinary life and guide you towards fulfilment and growth.

How to Use This Book

Feel free to explore different sections of the book that resonate with you in your current life journey. However, we believe that you will derive the greatest benefit by following the book chronologically and building your blueprint for high-performance living step by step.

By working through the book in order, you will establish a strong foundation for your personal growth and development. Each chapter builds upon the previous one, guiding you towards unlocking your potential and creating a life of extraordinary health, success, happiness and fulfilment.

Elevating your life doesn't just happen. Entrepreneurs, successful leaders, celebrities and athletes don't wake up one day having attained self-mastery, greatness or peak success. They understand that the ability to elevate life comes not from the fame they experience or how much money they make, but from within.

You are the leader of your own life – it is your responsibility and it starts with taking action. Leading yourself requires you to take a deep look at who you are, where you are going and how you will get there.

But this doesn't mean a massive overhaul of your life or investing a huge amount of energy. Instead, it requires daily focus on small conscious efforts and actions to unlock your potential and live a sustainable stunningly great life.

In our years of working with people from all walks of life – from sales assistants to parents, from start-up business owners to athletes and entrepreneurs – we have seen the power of the written word to shape our beliefs, thoughts and actions. Once you write something down – a goal, a plan, a habit, a list, a dream – you stoke the fire of motivation, you own it and your inspiration to do it doubles.

By creating intentional actions with the written word, you can unlock the extraordinary within you. This is why in each chapter there are breakout reflection sections where we'll ask what resonated with you and what actions you can 'stop, start and keep' to upgrade your performance and overall life.

Starting means taking that brave first step towards your goals, leaving behind doubts and complications. It's about turning intentions into actions and embarking on a purposeful journey.

Stopping involves letting go of things that hold you back – bad habits, negative thoughts, or anything that no longer serves you. This frees up space for growth and positive change.

Keeping is an ongoing commitment to excellence. It's about holding onto the habits, mindsets and actions that drive progress and bring you closer to your best life.

By embracing this 'stop, start, keep' approach, you'll find the clarity and power to transform your life. You'll simplify your path, ignite your potential, and rise from an ordinary existence to an extraordinary one, fuelled by purpose and passion. Being totally honest with the person in the mirror (your best friend, your unique self) is the starting point.

We've seen time and again the benefits of doing this inner work. Being willing to take action is the most important thing that separates those who are successful from those who aren't.

By the end of the book, you will have your own massive action plan – a clear vision and framework to kick-start you into fulfilment and growth. This plan will serve as your roadmap, giving you direction and motivation as you pursue high-performance living and success.

It is crucial to remember that by taking this step and embracing the power of committing your thoughts and intentions to paper is the key that unlocks the vault of your true potential.

The power of the written word

Expressing our thoughts through writing opens the door to a multitude of advantages:

▲ **Clarity:** It gives shape to our desires and intentions, providing a tangible representation of what we want to achieve. It brings clarity to our path and facilitates navigation towards our objectives.

▲ **Organisation:** It creates a framework for managing goals and allows us to visualise steps, break down tasks and prioritise effectively. With an organised plan, we stay focused, on track and steadily progress towards our desired outcomes.

▲ **Commitment:** It reinforces our dedication and accountability, and creates a visual reminder of our intentions, strengthening our commitment to take necessary steps. It compels us to honour those commitments, stay focused and take ownership of our responsibilities.

▲ **Memory:** It engages multiple brain areas, enhancing our retention of information and creates a written record we can refer to as needed. This documentation acts as a prompt and reminder, reducing the chances of forgetting tasks.

▲ **Motivation:** It gives us a roadmap to follow and keeps us motivated and energised.

▲ **Focus:** It enhances concentration and keeps us on track.

▲ **Prioritisation:** It makes it easier to evaluate the importance and urgency of each task. By prioritising our actions, we can make better use of our time and resources, ensuring that we tackle the most important tasks first.

▲ **Progress tracking:** It helps us track progress effectively. By documenting tasks and goals, we can assess the distance we've covered on our journey. It enables performance evaluation, milestone celebration and identification of necessary adjustments.

Whether you are a CEO, Olympic athlete, business owner, sales assistant, parent or teacher, this book will give you the skills you need to truly elevate your life, achieve outstanding results and create the life you want.

Do you want a masterplan for success? Are you ready to create the life you deserve? Then let's travel together on this transformative journey of human elevation. If you are committed to moving from ordinary to extraordinary, if you are willing to invest in yourself and create a future defined by greatness, then join us as we unlock the extraordinary within and elevate our lives together. The time for human elevation is now.

Your words have power. They shape and crystallise your beliefs, your thoughts, drive your behaviour and create your world.

Know the steps to elevate and create your personal action plan one action at a time for high-performance living.

Pillar 1

LIFE

Self-Awareness

Self-awareness is about truly knowing yourself and embracing ownership and empowerment in your journey. It means understanding your thoughts, emotions, strengths and weaknesses. Self-awareness is significant because it allows you to make conscious choices aligned with your values, empowering you to take control of your life. It helps you grow, recognise limiting beliefs and transform your life.

By cultivating self-awareness, you can live authentically and create positive change. It is a journey of self-discovery and personal empowerment where you embrace ownership of your choices and empower yourself to shape your own path.

Chapter 1

Discover Your Strengths

Knowing yourself is the
beginning of all wisdom

ARISTOTLE

Peak self-awareness starts with a crucial step: clarifying, focusing and utilising your unique set of character strengths. These strengths, acquired and shaped by your environment, experiences and the values you choose to embrace, form the very essence of your individual architecture. By delving into a thorough understanding of your strengths, you unlock your true potential and open the doors to an extraordinary life.

The Power of Your Strengths

When you become intimately acquainted with your strengths and leverage them effectively, you begin to thrive. This process allows you to live in a state of high flow, where you experience a harmonious alignment of your abilities, interests and the challenges you face. Flow is that state of complete immersion in an activity, where time seems to slip away and you feel fully absorbed and engaged in the present moment.

Creating more flow in your life becomes a transformative catalyst, generating a profound impact on your overall well-being. It is through the pursuit of activities and endeavours that elicit this state of flow that you unlock deeper levels of fulfilment as a human being – you become fully immersed in your passions, talents and the tasks that bring you joy and a sense of purpose.

The experience of flow allows you to tap into your inherent potential and push beyond your perceived limits. As you navigate your life with a heightened awareness of your strengths and seek opportunities that align with them, you uncover a greater sense of meaning and satisfaction, your actions become infused with purpose and the pursuit of your goals becomes a rewarding journey.

Embracing your unique strengths, leveraging them effectively and seeking out activities that elicit flow will bring about a state of heightened focus, creativity and productivity, and enable you to live a life that is deeply aligned with who you are at your core, fostering lasting happiness and a sense of purpose that transcends the ordinary.

Character strengths are not only the building blocks of flow and fulfilment, but also the positive personality traits that make you feel authentic and engaged. They are the essence of who you are, expressed through your feelings, behaviours and thoughts, creating your uniqueness. By cultivating awareness of your strengths, you establish a solid foundation for self-confidence, allowing you to embrace your true potential and navigate life with a sense of purpose.

Our strengths serve as a powerful reminder of how we are all individuals, each with our own unique combination of talents and qualities. They highlight the beauty of diversity and enable us to appreciate and celebrate our differences. Recognising and leveraging our strengths not only enhances our own lives, but also contributes to a harmonious and inclusive society that values and respects the strengths of others.

By nurturing an understanding of your character strengths, you unlock the transformative potential to shape your life in alignment with your authentic self.

We often see people trying to work on their flaws and shortcomings. There's no issue with this, but spending too much time focusing on our weaknesses can be demotivating and lead to low performance. In contrast to your strengths, your weaknesses drain you and can leave you feeling uninspired, depleted

Embrace your strengths, honour your individuality and embark on a remarkable journey towards self-discovery and personal satisfaction.

and tired – a great reason to avoid these wherever possible and not waste time on them. Science shows us that it is far more beneficial to focus on our strengths. In fact, it's estimated that it takes between 8,000 and 10,000 hours of practice to master a weakness. That's a couple of hours a day for ten to fourteen years!

Let's use our time more wisely and instead focus on elevating the best part of you – fine-tuning it and amplifying it for incredible results, both personally and professionally. When you know your strengths, you are gaining access to what you already have at your fingertips. With this insight you can align your career, hobbies and relationships in a way that has the greatest meaning, sustainability and purpose.

Character strengths are integral to the basic science of positive psychology. A strength or a character skill, when you are clear about how it serves you, is something you can work on and sharpen up to move forward faster. Defining your strengths will magnify your inner voice of power and lessen the voice of self-doubt and self-criticism. Knowledge is power and the power unleashed when you know your

> Our strengths are our internal compass; without any effort, they are there, ready for us to tap into to elevate our daily experiences and contribute to high-performance living.

strengths and have clarity will guide you to make the right decisions and take actions that enhance what already comes naturally to you. Gallup research found that people who use their strengths are up to six times more engaged in what they are doing and at least 10 per cent more productive. So, if you want to build high performance at work and create your dream career, focus on what you're good at, instead of what you're not.

Time and again, research has shown that knowing your strengths gives you a superpower of deep self-awareness empowering you to:

▲ Enhance confidence and self-belief.
▲ Gain clarity and direction.
▲ Amplify happiness and well-being.
▲ Foster stronger and more fulfilling relationships.
▲ Alleviate stress and promote resilience.
▲ Achieve personal and professional goals.
▲ Increase productivity and efficiency.
▲ Effectively navigate and overcome challenges.

How to Identify Your Character Strengths

Dr Martin Seligman at the University of Pennsylvania and the late Dr Chris Peterson at the University of Michigan found that twenty-four character strengths help people flourish.

Seligman and Peterson organised the character strengths into six principal virtues:

1. **Wisdom and Knowledge:** Cognitive strengths related to the acquisition and utilisation of information. Examples include creativity, open-mindedness and love of learning.
2. **Courage:** Strengths involving the determination to achieve objectives despite opposition – whether internal or external. Examples include bravery and perseverance.
3. **Humanity:** Strengths connected to caring for and befriending others. Examples include kindness and social intelligence.

4. **Justice:** Strengths that form the foundation of a thriving community life, with a focus on civic responsibility. Examples include teamwork and fairness.

5. **Temperance:** Strengths that provide protection against excess. Examples include humility and self-control.

6. **Transcendence:** Strengths that establish connections to the broader universe and confer meaning. Examples include an appreciation of beauty, hope and spirituality.

It is important to know that everyone possesses all twenty-four character strengths within the six virtues, but we have them show up in varying degrees in our life. They are a part of our unique identity and provide excitement, energy, clarity and authenticity. Your strengths can gradually change over time depending on what age and stage you are at in the life cycle.

> Strengths use is associated with improved performance, satisfaction and increased well-being.

Take a look at the list on the following page and identify what three words represent your strengths (the explanations are mostly taken from viacharacter.org). When working through this exercise, it might help to think about what three words your closest friends would choose to describe you. By defining your strengths you will then be able to take action. Without action we cannot elevate and live a life of exceptional results. You can also take the free online test that will uncover your twenty-four strengths in order of priority at viacharacter.org.

THE VIA CHARACTER STRENGTHS CHART

Circle your top three

Strength is bulit upon character.
Character is built upon inner strength.

Beauty and excellence Transcendence	**Bravery** Courage	**Creativity** Wisdom	**Curiosity** Wisdom
Fairness Justice	**Forgiveness** Temperance	**Gratitude** Transcendence	**Honesty** Courage
Hope Transcendence	**Humility** Temperance	**Humour** Transcendence	**Judgement** Wisdom
Kindness Humanity	**Leadership** Justice	**Love** Humanity	**Love of learning** Wisdom
Perseverance Courage	**Perspective** Wisdom	**Prudence** Temperance	**Self-regulation** Temperance
Social intelligence Humanity	**Spirituality** Transcendence	**Teamwork** Justice	**Zest** Courage

Appreciation of beauty and excellence (Transcendence)

You notice and appreciate beauty, excellence and people's skills. You don't take things for granted. You are responsive and feel awe and wonder at physical beauty (auditory, tactile or abstract) and at other skills and talents which energise you and inspire admiration and feelings of elevation.

Bravery (Courage)

You act with mental or physical strength even when you're afraid. You face rather than avoid your fears. Types of bravery are physical (firefighters, police officers), psychological (facing painful life events and aspects of oneself) and moral (speaking up for what is right). You act on your convictions in spite of challenges, threats and difficulties.

Creativity (Wisdom)

You come up with new ways to do and think about things. You conceptualise ideas that are useful and result in something worthwhile. There are two essential components to creativity: originality and adaptability.

Curiosity (Wisdom)

You like to explore and discover, and take an interest in anything and everything. Curiosity is often described as novelty-seeking and being open to experience and is associated with a natural desire to build knowledge. There are two components: you are interested in exploring new ideas, activities and experiences; and you have a strong desire to increase your personal knowledge.

Fairness (Justice)

You treat people justly and don't let your personal feelings bias your decisions about others. You want to give everyone a fair chance and believe there should be equal opportunity for all. You are also able to put yourself in somebody else's shoes and show empathy, kindness and compassion.

Forgiveness (Temperance)

You forgive those who have upset, wronged or hurt you. You accept that people make mistakes. You use this information in future relations with people on how to handle them and where to set boundaries. Forgiveness means letting go and also accepting others' shortcomings. Forgiveness is not about condoning, forgetting or reconciliation, but rather letting bygones be bygones.

Gratitude (Transcendence)

You are thankful for good things that happen. It involves feeling and expressing a deep sense of thankfulness in life and taking the time to genuinely express thankfulness to others. There are two stages of gratitude: acknowledging the goodness in your life; and recognising that the source of this goodness is outside yourself.

Honesty (Courage)

You speak the truth. You present yourself in a genuine and sincere way, without pretence, and take responsibility for your feelings and actions. You are a person of integrity – you are who you say you are – and you act consistently. Honesty is often linked to self-concordance – the extent to which your goals accurately represent your implicit interests and values.

Hope (Transcendence)

You have positive expectations for the future. Hope involves optimistic thinking and focusing on good things to come. It is more than a feel-good emotion. It is an action–orientated strength involving agency, and the motivation and confidence that goals can be reached.

Humility (Temperance)

You see your strengths and talents but are humble, not seeking to be the centre of attention or to receive recognition. You think well of yourself and have a good sense of who you are, and are aware of your mistakes and imperfections, but are content without being the centre of attention or getting praised for your accomplishments.

Humour (Transcendence)

You approach life playfully, making others smile or laugh and finding humour in difficult and stressful times. You are able to offer the lighter side to others. You are composed and cheerful and can sustain a good mood. Humour is seen as a valuable tool for coping with distressing situations.

Judgement (Wisdom)

You weigh all aspects objectively in making decisions, including arguments that are in conflict with your convictions. It involves making rational and logical choices, critical thinking, thinking things through and looking at evidence from all sides rather than jumping to conclusions.

Kindness (Humanity)

You are helpful, empathetic and regularly do nice favours for others without expecting anything in return. Kind people believe that others are worthy of attention and affirmation for their own sake as human beings, not out of a sense of duty. You have empathy, sympathy and moral reasoning and display social responsibility.

Leadership (Justice)

You take charge and guide groups to meaningful goals, and ensure good relations among group members. Effective leaders are able to provide a positive vision or message that inspires dedicated followers who feel empowered and perhaps even inspired. There are two types of leaders: transactional (clarify responsibilities, expectations, tasks) and transformational (motivate followers to perform at an extremely high level, fostering a climate of trust and commitment to the company and its goals).

Love (Humanity)

You experience close, loving relationships that are characterised by giving and receiving love, warmth and caring. You value close relationships with people and contribute to that closeness in a warm and genuine way. You are also willing to accept love. There are four types of love: attachment (parent and child); compassionate/ altruistic (kindness); companionate (friendship); and romantic (partner).

Love of learning (Wisdom)

You are motivated to acquire new levels of knowledge or deepen your existing knowledge or skills in a significant way. You love learning and are motivated by the expansion of your fund of knowledge.

Perseverance (Courage)

You persist towards your goals despite obstacles, discouragement or disappointments. Perseverance is sticking with things, being hard-working and finishing what is started, despite barriers that arise. You can dig deep and muster the will to overcome thoughts of giving up. As you complete things, you build confidence for future successes and goal accomplishment. Perseverance requires both effort for a task and duration to keep up the task.

Perspective (Wisdom)

You have the ability to see the bigger picture in life. You can see the forest as well as the trees, and avoid getting wrapped up in the small details when there are bigger issues to consider. While listening to others, perspective helps you to simultaneously think about life lessons, proper conduct and what's best for the situation being discussed.

Prudence (Temperance)

You act carefully and cautiously, looking to avoid unnecessary risks and planning with the future in mind. Prudence is a strength of restraint and you are able to consider the long-term consequences of your actions. It is a form of practical reasoning, the ability to examine the potential consequences and to control yourself based on that examination. It is often referred to as cautious wisdom, practical wisdom and practical reason.

Self-regulation (Temperance)

You manage your feelings and actions and are disciplined and self-controlled. Self-regulation is about controlling your appetites and emotions and regulating what you do. You have a good level of confidence that you are likely to achieve your goals. It helps you keep a sense of balance, order and progress, and is a resource that can be depleted and fatigued. It acts as a muscle that can be exhausted through overexertion or strengthened through regular practice.

Social intelligence (Humanity)

You are aware of and understand your feelings and thoughts as well as the feelings of those around you. You know what makes other people tick, are aware of the motives and feelings of yourself and others, and know how to fit into different social situations. There are two components to social intelligence: social awareness (what we sense about others) and social facility (what we do with our awareness).

Spirituality (Transcendence)

You feel spiritual and believe in a sense of purpose or meaning in your life. You see your place in the grand scheme of the universe and find meaning in everyday life. Spirituality involves the belief that there is a dimension to life that is beyond human understanding. It is universal and all cultures have a concept of an ultimate transcendent sacred force.

Teamwork (Justice)

You are a helpful and contributing group and team member and feel responsible for helping the team reach its goals. Teamwork means you are committed to contributing to the team's success. You are dedicated and reliable, and this can be in a friendship group, marriage, sporting team, business unit or small team working on a project together. Teamwork is closely related to three other concepts: citizenship (community); loyalty (trust for a group); and patriotism (loyalty to homeland without hostility towards other nations).

Zest (Courage)

You feel vital and full of energy. You approach life feeling activated and enthusiastic. You are excited to get up in the morning and live your life like an adventure. Zest is a dynamic strength that is directly related to physical and psychological wellness. This strength has the strongest ties to overall life satisfaction and a life of engagement.

Take action

Get clear, get confident and prioritise your unique strengths.

Once you know, own and connect with your character strengths, say them out loud and ask yourself some simple questions:

▲ What are your most powerful combinations of strengths?
▲ Do your strengths match up with those used in your job?
▲ What situations do your strengths naturally play out in?
▲ What strengths do you forget about when you are at your worst?
▲ When you last felt in flow, what strengths were you using?
▲ How can you make the most of your strengths by using them in new situations?

Elevate Your Strengths

What separates high performance and success from one human to another is the remarkable ability to not only recognise their strengths, but also harness them effectively to deliver exceptional results that align with their aspirations and goals. It is the understanding that strengths are not simply innate talents, but valuable resources that, when utilised skilfully, have the power to elevate performance and create a significant impact. High performers recognise the unique combination of strengths they possess and actively leverage them to push beyond boundaries, overcome challenges and consistently deliver outstanding outcomes. They strive to cultivate a deep understanding of their strengths, continually refine and develop them, and intentionally apply them in pursuit of their highest aspirations. It is through this deliberate utilisation of strengths that they unlock their full potential and achieve extraordinary levels of success and fulfilment. And you, too, can do the same.

One action you can take is to seek opportunities that allow you to utilise and enhance your strengths. This might involve taking on new projects or responsibilities that align with your strengths, seeking mentorship or training in areas where your strengths can be applied or finding ways to integrate your strengths into your daily activities.

As you consciously develop your strengths, you will begin to experience positive outcomes. You will feel a sense of fulfilment and engagement as you leverage your strengths to overcome challenges and achieve meaningful goals. Your confidence and self-belief will grow as you witness the impact you can make by utilising your strengths. Additionally, developing your strengths can lead to increased productivity, effectiveness and success in various areas of your life, whether that's your career, relationships or personal growth.

By developing your strengths with conscious awareness, you are investing in your personal growth and maximising your potential.

You are shaping a life that is aligned with your innate talents and passions, allowing you to thrive and make a positive impact. So, embrace the journey of developing your strengths, and unlock the limitless possibilities it holds for your elevated life:

- ▲ **Focus on your top three strengths:** Identify and prioritise your key strengths, dedicating time and effort to harness and leverage them in your personal and professional life.
- ▲ **Develop new skills to elevate your strengths:** Continuously seek out opportunities for growth and learning, acquiring new skills that complement and enhance your existing strengths.
- ▲ **Maintain balance with your strengths:** While emphasising your strengths, remember to maintain a balanced approach by also addressing areas that require improvement or development.
- ▲ **Utilise your strengths for high performance:** Apply your strengths intentionally and strategically, maximising their potential to achieve exceptional performance and success in your endeavours.

High-performing individuals understand the power of acknowledging their strengths and making them a visible part of their daily life. To align with your strengths and live with purpose and intention, create a habit of writing them down and ensuring you look at them regularly. You can incorporate them into your daily routine by setting them as a screen saver, recording them in your journal or seeking out quotes that resonate with your strengths.

The benefits of professional strength work

In the world of high performance, leaders will combine strengths such as teamwork, humour, fairness and honesty to take teams to the height of their success. Everyone in the team will bring their own individual strengths to elevate the team to success.

For example, a leader with 'honesty' will value giving constructive feedback to the team but may need to temper this slightly to not be hurtful. A leader with 'teamwork' may embed rituals such as shaking hands, high-fiving or celebration moments to keep morale high in the team. A leader with 'self-regulation' may use this in role modelling self-control when faced with a host of seemly unfair events out of their control.

Character strengths such as hope, perseverance, bravery and zest are a few strengths that, when habituated in an elite athlete, provide the greatest opportunity to improve performance, enjoyment and deliver outstanding world-class results. An athlete who has developed these strengths can call on the foundation of well-formed habits to support them in aspiring to true self-mastery and excellence.

Be Aware of the Shadow Side

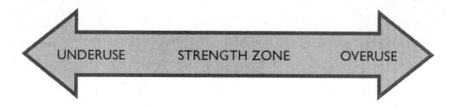

UNDERUSE   STRENGTH ZONE   OVERUSE

Be aware that your strengths have what researchers call a 'shadow side'. When we overuse, or overplay, a character strength, we tip the scales from this strength being beneficial and delivering high-performance results, to being harmful and self-sabotaging. Like many things in life, when we take something to the extreme, it can go from being a positive to a negative. Aristotle's work on virtues defines the 'Golden Mean' – where courage sits perfectly between the deficiency of cowardice and the excess of being overly rash – which underlines the idea that strengths should be used in just the right amount: not too much and not too little.

We all have a tendency to sometimes overuse our strengths to our detriment: be it too much 'kindness' that can leave us burnt out, neglecting our own needs and sacrificing personal growth, or too much 'hope' that can have us overcommitting.

You may find yourself overusing one of your strengths or using it in the wrong context or in a manipulative way:

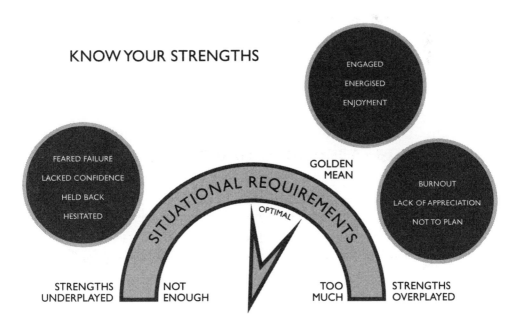

KNOW YOUR STRENGTHS

ENGAGED
ENERGISED
ENJOYMENT

FEARED FAILURE
LACKED CONFIDENCE
HELD BACK
HESITATED

GOLDEN MEAN

BURNOUT
LACK OF APPRECIATION
NOT TO PLAN

SITUATIONAL REQUIREMENTS

OPTIMAL

STRENGTHS UNDERPLAYED

NOT ENOUGH

TOO MUCH

STRENGTHS OVERPLAYED

Here are some examples:

▲ **A high achiever (+), but unable to enjoy the moment (-):** learn to be more mindful.

▲ **Energetic (+), but restless and anxious (-):** embrace the pace.

▲ **Highly adaptable (+), but lack structure and consistency (-):** create basic plans.

▲ **Kindness (+), people take advantage of you (-):** set some boundaries.

▲ **Self-regulation (+), become obsessed, rigid (-):** find some flexibility.

▲ **Humility (+), conceal feelings of self-worth (-):** celebrate with others.

By consistently reinforcing your strengths, you can cultivate a mindset that allows you to leverage them effectively while remaining mindful of their shadow side. For example, if 'honesty' is one of your strengths, it is important to exercise discernment, ensuring that your honesty is delivered tactfully and considerately, taking into account the feelings and sensitivities of others. This practice empowers you to embrace your strengths authentically and unlock your full potential for success.

Take action

▲ How is overusing your strengths detrimental to your success?

▲ In what aspects of your life do you take your strengths to extremes that are harmful to you?

▲ How can you use your strengths in a healthier and more balanced, high-performance way?

If you want to stand out, supercharge your life and propel your career, believe deep down that you can improve, elevate and master your strengths, making them work for you every single day. Once you start flexing your strengths, that's when the magic starts to happen, and you'll be amazed at the difference it makes to your professional and personal life.

Shannah: My strengths are honesty, appreciation of beauty and excellence, and self-regulation. When I focused on understanding, really defining and living my strengths, my level of self-awareness increased and I could see clearly when overplay came in and self-sabotage appeared. For example, I was always told I was a straight shooter, but I've learnt to notice when I have to bring my answers back a little so as not to offend people.

I relish in appreciation of beauty and excellence in the smallest of details, and focusing further on this has enhanced my life in every way possible. It has also led to me living a much more mindful life, noticing the small things that really mean the most rather than racing past the beauty that is all around me.

Not paying attention to self-regulation led to burnout, chronic fatigue and depression as I was a master of using hard work and commitment as a badge of honour. The gift was to learn to find the sweet spot, to be able to pull back slightly to avoid sabotaging my own health, both mentally and physically.

I have spent time working on these top three strengths, really delving into them, thinking about them, feeling them, seeing them daily on the mirror in whiteboard marker, connecting with them, understanding them and finally using them to elevate my life both personally and professionally.

Strengths summary

1. Strengths focus on what you are already good at.
2. Fine-tune and upgrade your focus on your strengths, not your weaknesses.
3. You hit a state of flow when using your strengths.
4. Beware of overusing your strengths resulting in self-sabotage.
5. Develop your strengths with conscious awareness to elevate your life.

Create Your Personal High-Performance Plan: STRENGTHS

Write three words that represent your strengths:

1. _____
2. _____
3. _____

To elevate your strengths:

What do you need to STOP doing?

1. _____
   _____
2. _____
   _____
3. _____
   _____

What do you need to START doing?

1. _____
   _____
2. _____
   _____
3. _____
   _____

What do you need to KEEP doing?

1. _____
   _____
2. _____
   _____
3. _____
   _____

Chapter 2

Embrace Your Values

Values dictate your
evaluations, decisions and
actions which create your
destiny . . . they act
as your compass

TONY ROBBINS

Have you ever made decisions but knew deep down they were not right, but you went ahead anyway only to find yourself miserable or somewhere where you didn't want to be? Unfortunately, many people coast through life without any consideration of what is truly and deeply important to them; life just happens 'to' them. They may feel trapped, frustrated or stuck with their decisions and results, knowing they are not reaching their potential or experiencing happiness and fulfilment in their daily lives. In high-performance living this is called mediocrity – making decisions with no clarity, solid foundations, defined code of conduct or roadmap to follow.

An important part of playing your A-game in leadership or life is making sure your daily actions and activities reflect your values. Values show you who you are and provide a framework for your actions, reactions and interactions, and the decisions you make. Compromising on your values catches up with you and can have catastrophic results, undermining your authenticity and personal fulfilment. It is essential to stay true to yourself and your values, fostering a sense of inner harmony and genuine connections with others.

In today's world many people have become very influenced by advertising, social media and peer group pressure, and fall into the trap of defining themselves and their true worth and what is most important to them by comparison to others. Individuals measure their own success, achievements or self-worth based on the accomplishments, possessions or social status of others. For instance, someone might feel inadequate or

> High-performance living is to live, lead and love with authenticity, passion and purpose. Values influence your personal attitude, outlooks and behaviours.

unsuccessful because they don't have the same material possessions as their peers, or they may undervalue their own abilities because they perceive others as more accomplished in a particular field. This constant comparison can lead to a sense of dissatisfaction, self-doubt and an inability to appreciate one's own unique strengths and values.

If you want to do things differently, welcome to your journey of personal self-discovery. A life of simple, well-defined values is a life of self-respect, dignity, integrity, authenticity and confidence. To elevate your experience of life and make high-performance decisions, you need to clearly define what is most important to you personally, free from external influences.

Acknowledging and understanding your own set of values offers protection from the barrage of external influences and brings a sense of heightened empowerment. The old saying of 'stay in your own lane' or 'keep your eyes on your own plate' helps us stay laser-focused on our own life journey.

Core values are the key to true high performance.

Why values take you to world-class decision-making

Your values:

▲ Guide your habits, social experience and lifestyle choices.
▲ Define your self-worth and steer you in the right direction for long-term fulfilment.
▲ Serve as the foundation for confidence.
▲ Future-proof your long-terms plans.
▲ Are the gateway to your authentic self.
▲ Give you purpose in your day-to-day living.
▲ Help you clear the clutter and live with clarity.
▲ Guide your reactions in difficult situations.

Identifying Your Core Values

Your values are a fundamental part of self-awareness. They are defined by what's most important in your life, deep in your soul – the ideas and beliefs you consider most significant. Our values give us clarity and confidence in decision-making and ultimately help us live a happy and successful life.

For a moment, we want you to think of yourself as a babushka doll: the outer doll is the face you wear and the personality you present to the world. We want you to dig deeper than this surface-level representation and keep opening the doll, one layer after another, until you get right to the core.

Values are your lighthouse. They are signals giving you direction, meaning and purpose, and protect you from compromising who you are.

Who are you really? Who are you without your job title, without the hats you wear, the roles you play, the identity markers you have become so attached to? It is a confronting exercise as many people will define themselves by their title or job: parent, assistant, business owner, CEO, athlete, coach, lawyer, accountant, entrepreneur, and so on. But this is simply what you do, not who you are at the core of your being. If we take away the titles, who are you and what is most important to you?

Below are some thought-starters for discovering more about your values and elevating your self-awareness muscle. Remember, high performance comes from clarity, answering questions, going in deep, finding your truth and putting in the work.

Take action

▲ What is most important to you?

▲ If you could change one thing in your life, what would it be?

▲ Who or what inspires you?

▲ What are you afraid of?

▲ What are you putting up with?

▲ What are you truly passionate about?

▲ What do you really want for your future?

▲ What has been your biggest life lesson?

Values evolve

Throughout your life, you have likely been influenced by various individuals such as mentors, teachers and family members, each with their own set of values. As you navigate through different stages and experiences, you might have incorporated some of these values into your own belief system. For example, during your high-school years, you may have embraced values like achievement, learning or social connection. As you progressed into your professional life, you might have adopted values such as integrity, ambition or innovation. In retirement, your values might shift towards relaxation, fulfilment or giving back to the community. Your personal values are influenced by these external factors and can undergo transformations, reflecting your growth and evolving understanding of what truly matters to you.

It is important to reflect on your values and evaluate whether they still align with your authentic self as you continue your journey through life. What held great significance to us during our high-school years may no longer resonate with us at the height of our careers or during retirement. As we grow and evolve, our values naturally shift, reflecting our changing priorities, experiences and aspirations. It is crucial to acknowledge that our roadmap, guided by our values, also needs to be regularly updated to align with our evolving selves. By recognising and embracing the morphing nature of our values, we can navigate life's journey with authenticity, purpose and a true reflection of who we are in the present moment.

How to define your personal set of values:

Achievement	Environment	Learning
Advancement	Equality	Legacy
Adventure	Fairness	Love
Affection	Faith	Loyalty
Authenticity	Fame	Nature
Authority	Family	Openness
Autonomy	Financial security	Optimism
Balance	Forgiveness	Order
Beauty	Freedom	Peace
Boldness	Friendship	Personal development
Career	Fun	Pleasure
Challenge	Generosity	Popularity
Change	Gratitude	Power
Comfort	Growth	Recognition
Communication	Happiness	Relationships
Community	Health	Religion
Compassion	Honesty	Reputation
Competition	Humanity	Respect
Connection	Humour	Responsibility
Contribution	Influence	Self-respect
Cooperation	Inner harmony	Spirituality
Creativity	Inspiration	Stability
Culture	Integrity	Status
Curiosity	Involvement	Success
Determination	Justice	Teamwork
Discipline	Kindness	Trust
Empathy	Knowledge	Wealth
Energy	Leadership	Wisdom

Step 1: Identify

Look at the list opposite and identify your top ten values, then rank them in order of importance, with 1 being the most important:

1. _____
2. _____
3. _____
4. _____
5. _____
6. _____
7. _____
8. _____
9. _____
10. _____

Step 2: Prioritise

Prioritise the top five values that clearly reflect what is most important to you:

1. _____
2. _____
3. _____
4. _____
5. _____

Step 3: Define

Write down the top three values that are fundamentally most important in your life, support your decision-making and sit as your lighthouse:

1. _____
2. _____
3. _____

Step 4: Reflect

Reflect on the meaning of these three values. How do these values make you feel? How do they sit in your deep core?

Reflect deeply on your top three values and write what they mean to you personally:

1. _____

_____

_____

2. _____

_____

_____

3. _____

_____

_____

Step 5: Take Action

Like high-performance athletes, individuals, family units, teams or corporations, it is crucial to translate your values into action. Make a pledge to yourself and commit to living your values every day. Take the time to write them down, for the written word holds immense power.

By actively engaging with your values, integrating them into your thoughts, actions and decisions, you create a strong internal compass that guides you towards success. Embrace the opportunity to see, live, breathe and connect with your values on a daily basis, allowing them to shape your path to achievement.

How to keep your values top of mind to elevate self-awareness

▲ Write them down.

▲ Put a Post-it note on your car dashboard.

▲ Write them on your mirror in whiteboard marker.

▲ Have them next to your bed.

▲ Program them as your screen saver.

▲ Put them in as a daily reminder on your devices.

▲ Display them on the fridge.

▲ Create a visual in words or pictures and hang it up so you can see it daily.

How to Use Values in Daily Life

Now that you know your values, it is time to own them, fine-tune them and live your life through them. For example:

Family

If family is one of your values but you:

▲ Work sixty hours a week.

▲ Are too tired to spend intimate or quality time with your partner.

▲ Often find yourself on a screen, multitasking while in the presence of your kids.

▲ Never switch off and enjoy time with your family.

Consider:

- ▲ Prioritising quality time: Dedicate time for meaningful activities with your partner and children, being fully present.
- ▲ Setting work boundaries: Create a healthier work–life balance by reassessing commitments, establishing clearer boundaries and making time for your family.
- ▲ Practising mindful technology use: Limit screen time, create tech-free zones and prioritise face-to-face interactions to foster connection and reduce distractions.

What can you do?

Health

If health is a value but you:

- ▲ Don't eat whole food and opt for fast or packaged foods.
- ▲ Don't prioritise getting enough sleep each night.
- ▲ Don't have time to exercise because you are too 'busy' or 'tired'.
- ▲ Don't prioritise mini pauses to breathe properly or meditate or journal.

Consider:

- ▲ Choosing nutritious foods: Prioritise nutritious fresh food options over fast or packaged foods.
- ▲ Prioritising restful sleep: Establish a bedtime routine that promotes quality sleep.

▲ Making time for physical activity: Incorporate regular physical activity into your schedule, choosing activities that you enjoy.

What can you do?

Achievement

If achievement is a value but you:

▲ Find it hard to get started on new things because you get distracted often.
▲ Don't put yourself forward for promotions, awards or new opportunities.
▲ Commit to too many projects or goals at once and never manage to complete them.
▲ Just hope for the best without writing anything down.

Consider:

▲ Overcoming distractions: Develop strategies to stay focused and minimise distractions when starting new tasks.
▲ Embracing opportunities: Take proactive steps to put yourself forward for promotions and new opportunities that align with your goals and aspirations.
▲ Effective goal-setting: Set clear and concise goals and create a plan of action to increase your chances of achieving them (see Chapter 11 for more on goal-setting).

What can you do?

Beware the pitfalls of perfectionism

In the pursuit of achievement, we can easily fall into the trap of perfectionism, leading to stress, anxiety and low self-confidence. Break free from this mindset and redefine healthy achievement beyond mere goal-smashing or material gains.

If trapped in perfectionism, pause and refuel. Disconnect from technology, practise mindfulness through meditation and cherish quality time with loved ones. This holistic approach embodies true high-performance living, prioritising self-care and meaningful connections.

Embracing a healthier perspective on achievement cultivates a fulfilling and sustainable path to personal growth. Remember to enjoy the journey and create a balanced, purposeful life.

Wealth

If wealth is a value but you:

▲ Don't have a savings or financial plan.
▲ Don't respect money by staying up to date on bills and budgets.
▲ Spend more than you earn.
▲ Waste money buying things you don't really need.

Consider:

▲ Assessing your current financial situation: Determine your income, expenses and debt level.
▲ Analysing your spending patterns: Identify areas where you can cut back.
▲ Educating yourself by reading books, attending seminars or seeking financial advice from a trusted expert or source.

What can you do?

Self-respect

If self-respect is a value but you:

▲ Constantly talk down to yourself undermining your self-worth.

▲ Battle persistent and negative thoughts that hinder your self-esteem.

▲ Fail to stand up for yourself in personal and professional situations.

▲ Question your worthiness and doubt whether you are 'good enough'.

Consider:

▲ Challenging your negative thoughts: Replace them with positive affirmations.

▲ Celebrating your small wins: Focus on your accomplishments to build your confidence muscle.

▲ Engaging in hobbies or voluntary work that boost your self-esteem and give fulfilment.

What can you do?

By honestly questioning your values in this way and asking what you can stop, start and keep, you can identify areas for growth and take proactive steps to a more fulfilling and empowered life.

Remember, nothing changes if nothing changes!

Using your values for decision-making

Your values are your lighthouse and will guide you in making the right decisions. Use them when asking yourself . . .

▲ Should I accept this job opportunity?
▲ Do I want to follow tradition or travel down a new path?
▲ Is this relationship good for me?
▲ Should I compromise or be firm on my position?
▲ Is this risk worth taking?
▲ Why am I not achieving the goals I have set for myself?

Organisational values

Organisational values serve as guiding principles that shape an organisation's culture, behaviour and decision-making. They embody the beliefs and principles that define an organisation's identity and guide its actions.

Below are some examples of organisational values:

▲ **Integrity:** Acting with honesty, transparency and ethical behaviour in all aspects of business.
▲ **Innovation:** Encouraging creativity, embracing change and fostering a culture of continuous improvement.
▲ **Collaboration:** Promoting teamwork, open communication and cooperation among employees and stakeholders.
▲ **Customer-centricity:** Putting the needs and satisfaction of customers at the centre of all operations and decision-making.
▲ **Respect:** Treating individuals with dignity, valuing diversity and maintaining a supportive work environment.
▲ **Excellence:** Striving for high standards of quality, professionalism and continuous learning.

▲ **Accountability:** Taking ownership of actions, meeting commitments and being responsible for results.

▲ **Sustainability:** Incorporating environmentally friendly practices, social responsibility and long-term thinking.

▲ **Adaptability:** Embracing flexibility, agility and the ability to respond to dynamic market conditions.

▲ **Empowerment:** Encouraging autonomy and trust, and providing opportunities for personal and professional growth.

Values have a powerful impact in your life, both personal and professional. They provide you with four main high-performance drivers: direction, certainty, momentum and fulfilment. They get you moving, tell you what to pay attention to each day and make your goals (which we'll explore a bit later – see Chapter 11) meaningful. When you succeed through your values, you experience a deep sense of fulfilment, energy and excitement in victory. Know your values. Change your story. Take action. Elevate your life.

Colleen: As part of my toolkit for recovery from burnout I decided to get myself a life coach. And that person was Shannah. At our first session, she asked me two questions: who am I and what are my values? I had no idea how to answer either question.

I didn't know who I was without my job, without the hats I wore, the roles I played, and, although I was crystal clear on the organisational values, I certainly hadn't identified my own values – which is why and how I had ended up in this place of burnout. It was clear I had a lot of work to do . . . on myself!

I soon identified that one of my values was health. Clarifying this value as a top priority highlighted many things I needed to stop, start and keep in my life. I needed to build in self-care, set boundaries, share the load and learn to say 'no' more often. Identifying and pledging my values allowed me to build habits into my life that would better serve me (and those around me).

Even today, many years later, health is still at the top of my priority list and is an essential aspect of the way I live my life.

Values summary

1. Personal values are a foundational part of high-performance living and self-awareness.
2. Values give you clarity, purpose and direction.
3. Values guide your habits and lifestyle choices.
4. Values are your most powerful decision-making tools.
5. Values guide your decisions for high-performance living.

Create Your Personal High-Performance Plan: VALUES

Write three words that represent your top values:

1. _____
2. _____
3. _____

To elevate your values:

What do you need to STOP doing?

1. _____
   _____
2. _____
   _____
3. _____
   _____

What do you need to START doing?

1. _____
   _____
2. _____
   _____
3. _____
   _____

What do you need to KEEP doing?

1. _____
   _____
2. _____
   _____
3. _____
   _____

Chapter 3

Create Your Vision and Roadmap

Vision without action is a daydream. Action without vision is a nightmare

JAPANESE PROVERB

Many people don't have a vision. They cannot think about what they want for their future as they are just living life and reacting to the daily circumstances they find themselves in. This feeling can be compared to being in the passenger seat of life, rather than in the driver's seat, or just going around the roundabout, over and over again, not knowing when or where to exit. They find each year just seems to be on repeat with no changes, no growth, no excitement, no acceleration. The price of no vision is a feeling of stagnation, stuck energy, not moving, not growing, frustration, stuck on the old treadmill of life, mediocrity and doing the same old things while watching others around you excel.

Creating a personal vision gives you clarity, purpose and direction for everyday living. It takes your strengths, inspiration, compassion, values, ambition and creativity as a reference point for all of your decision-making in leadership and in life. It opens your mind, fuels your fire and enables you to create a roadmap for your future to keep you motivated and inspired to be your best self.

You need a roadmap for success in both your professional and personal life. An example we see in many professional athletes is they have a clear and concise vision for their careers but lack a vision for their personal lives, leaving them feeling lost and disillusioned when they are in their off season, suffer injury or don't make the team. We all need a personal and professional vision for high-impact and high-performance living.

Why Having a Vision Is Important

A personal vision is your GPS system for life. It is not just a picture of what you could be or what you want, it's a call-out to your better self to become something more in life. It dares you to dream, set goals and elevate your habits to create the life you deserve. Defining a powerful, motivating and inspiring vision that is packed with purpose and is in alignment with your strengths, values and intentions will elevate you in your life journey.

Your life vision defines who you want to be, what you want to be known for and the set of experiences and accomplishments you are aiming to achieve. Your vision will help you create a framework to set goals and powerful actions to achieve your future vision.

By creating a personal vision, you tap into the profound understanding of your 'why', igniting a deep sense of meaning and fulfilment in your life, as you realise the true purpose behind your actions and the impact you can make in the world around you.

When you fire up and get creative you can then design your life and your plan and take massive action. Your brain is equipped with a plan, a pathway, a roadmap and now it can ignite, rise up, get going and kick goals.

> Know and own where you are going.

You don't have to be best in the world, but you can be the best in your own race. Don't lose your magic that makes you special or give up on your dreams. Let's instead ignite them and design your roadmap for success. Your dreams are the highest expression of your inner self, and open the doorway for you to create a vision that lights you up. The world needs heroes and people to aspire to; people delivering on their dreams, creating amazing things, breaking through glass ceilings and living a life of fulfilment and success.

Those who set aside time to clarify and amplify their vision and allow themselves to be limitless will achieve greatness. After all, where your focus goes your energy flows. So get clear, dream big and take action! Your dreams are the highest expression of your exceptional self.

Create Your Personal Five-Year Vision

So where do you want to go, how do you want to get there and what does it look like? Do you want to make the rest of your life the most productive, exciting and satisfying years you've ever had? Start with a five-year plan.

Five years is 260 weeks, 1,826 days, 2,629,440 minutes. What could you do in this time?

1. Write down your age in five years' time.
2. Write down your partner's/children's ages in five years' time.
3. Write down your parents'/pets' ages in five years' time.

Now you will see that in five years' time your life will look different. The landscape will be changed, your body will be different, your children will be older and your current circumstances and commitments will have evolved. Nothing stays the same. Everything changes, so embrace, prepare and plan for the change.

Start thinking about:

A vision is not just a picture of what could be, it is an appeal to our better selves, a call to become something more.

▲ How you want to feel.
▲ How you see yourself living and working.
▲ What experiences you want.
▲ What you want to learn.

▲   Where you want to be financially.

▲   What challenges you want to have conquered.

Have clarity, be bold and dream big. Remember a vague vision will give you a vague result. Your vision is your responsibility!

Take action

The more clarity you have the easier it is for you to set goals and achieve your future vision. Explore the thought-starters below to gain clarity on the desired vision for your life five years from now.

Personal vision thought-starters

In five years' time, define:

How you want to feel physically, mentally and emotionally

Physically: Energetic, vibrant and strong.

Mentally: Clear-minded, focused and resilient.

Emotionally: Balanced, content and emotionally intelligent.

Where you are at on your wealth creation strategy

Saving a portion of income regularly.

Diversifying investments to minimise risk.

Working towards paying off debts and managing expenses effectively.

Your living environment

Organised and clutter-free space.

Surrounded by items that bring joy and inspiration.

A comfortable and peaceful atmosphere that promotes well-being.

How your relationships and networks have evolved
> *Cultivating meaningful and supportive friendships.*
> *Building a network of like-minded individuals or mentors.*
> *Strengthening relationships with family members.*

The habits you want to have mastered
> *Consistent exercise routine.*
> *Regular practice of mindfulness or meditation.*
> *Reading or learning something new daily.*

Your state of confidence and your motivation for life
> *Feeling self-assured and believing in your abilities.*
> *Embracing challenges as opportunities for growth.*
> *Finding purpose and inspiration in everyday life.*

Professional vision thought-starters

In five years' time, define:
The skill sets you want to improve
> *Effective communication and public speaking.*
> *Financial literacy and investment strategies.*
> *Digital marketing or technological proficiency.*

Who you want to have as a mentor
> *Industry experts or leaders in your field of interest.*
> *Successful entrepreneurs or business professionals.*
> *Established artists or creatives in your desired field.*

Who is in your high-performance network
> *Motivated and driven individuals who inspire and challenge you.*
> *Thought leaders or influencers in your field of interest.*
> *Individuals from diverse backgrounds and perspectives.*

What you ultimately want to have accomplished

Launching your own business or start-up.

Attaining financial independence or financial freedom.

Making a positive impact in your community or society.

How people will describe you

Resilient and adaptable.

Inspiring and motivating.

Visionary and innovative.

How you define success

Continuous growth and learning.

Making a positive impact on others and the world.

Having a balanced and harmonious lifestyle.

Watch the world open as you reach great heights of success, fulfilment and happiness after doing this activity.

Write it out

You now have a clear picture of what you want to create: ideas, inspirations, direction, words and perspective of how your life will be evolved in five years' time. Write a few paragraphs to capture this information and explore how you want to feel, look and act. Write as if it is actually happening, in the present tense. This will connect you emotionally with where you want to go.

We have provided an example of a life experience vision on the following page to inspire you:

Life experiences have enriched my journey in profound ways. Five years from now, my life is an exquisite tapestry of cherished memories, adventures and personal growth. I have actively sought out new experiences, stepping out of my comfort zone with enthusiasm and curiosity. I have travelled to captivating destinations, immersing myself in different cultures and expanding my horizons. Meaningful connections with diverse individuals have deepened my understanding of the world and broadened my perspective. Each experience has contributed to my personal evolution, shaping me into a more compassionate, open-minded and enlightened individual.

Create a vision board

A vision board is a visual representation of how you would like your life to look. It is a high-performance tool to help you visualise your goals and activate the law of attraction. Instantly through pictures you bring your goals top of mind, and you will subconsciously look for ways to move closer to them.

The main idea of a vision board is that it is a central place where you capture inspirational images of your goals, the habits you want to create, the life experiences you want, the things you want to own, how you want to feel and what you want to do. This is the start of developing and building the life you want to live in.

Cut out pictures for your board or use sites like Pinterest to create visuals of your life map. Use words, affirmations, goal statements, your values, your strengths, pictures of places you want to travel to, the car you want to own, your business dreams, visuals of your health aspirations, living spaces, new adventures, family, friends, bucket list items, holiday homes, hobbies, retreat destinations and pictures that inspire your future self and represent how you want to feel and the elevated life you want to create.

Take your time to ensure the words on your vision board are powerful and reflect your future self. Make sure you can see your values and strengths clearly and that the pictures sing to you and spark feelings and emotion when you look at them. Connect emotionally to what you want to create for yourself:

▲   Do you really want it?
▲   Are you passionate about it?
▲   Does it create excitement for you and inspire you to take action?

When complete, put your vision board somewhere you can see it daily. Many take a photo of the finished product and save it as their screen saver.

Once your board is up:

▲   Look at it regularly for a daily dose of inspiration.
▲   Say the power words or quotes that inspire you out loud.
▲   Visualise yourself living the life your board represents.

Practise visualisation

Visualise, believe, achieve. Visualisation is a high-performance mental rehearsal skill and habit to practise. It prepares and teaches you how to respond to a situation before it happens. It also conditions your brain to see, hear and feel success in your mind. When you visualise, your imagination is walking through the scenarios as if rehearsing for a performance. It involves not just closing your eyes and seeing yourself accomplish the vision and goals, but feeling it also.

High-performance athletes use visualisation to achieve peak performance. They create mental images of training, the competition, the day of the event and think of the things and feelings they want. Visualisation is not just for elite athletes; it is for everyone, including you. Whether you are a student, entrepreneur, parent, business owner or sales assistant, visualisation, when combined with hard work, commitment, passion and practice, will result in world-class results.

If you want to start a business, you can close your eyes and visualise what it would be like to create the product and bring it to market. You would home in on the detail of each step, from conception to completion and really feel the experience and hear the applause when it is realised. If you want to visit the Maldives, you can close your eyes, visualise the blue sea, the villa, and feel the heat of the sun, smell the salt water and imagine tasting the cocktail.

All our dreams start with having a future vision!

Creative Visualisation

Decide on a target

Use all your senses

Stay calm and pay attention

Think positively

Three High-Performance Steps for Outstanding Results

Step 1: Create momentum

Start by examining your habits and daily activities to ensure they support your aspirations. Evaluate how you spend your time and who you surround yourself with, as they can significantly impact your progress. Take a moment to consider what small step you can take today to move closer to your desired outcome. By consistently making conscious choices and taking meaningful action, you can create momentum and experience a greater sense of achievement.

Step 2: Develop your vision habit

Your vision is an ever-evolving dream. It is to be nurtured, protected, cared for and reviewed yearly. It will change and evolve and grow as you do. Each year the landscape of your life will change and sometimes life throws you curveballs or opportunities you didn't see coming. Your environment changes, family dynamics change, your body changes and the doors to possibility change as new people enter your life. The key to success is to stay committed to achieving your goals and fine-tuning your habits on a regular basis.

Step 3: Share your dreams

Share your vision with those you trust so they can support you, fuel your energy, give you drive, strength and belief, so you are unstoppable in your pursuit to elevating your life and unleashing your incredible power within.

Create Your Professional Five-Year Vision

A powerful professional vision goes beyond a simple statement, transforming into a vibrant and inspiring picture of the future. This vision is filled with images, symbols, words, quotes, goals and stories that paint a clear roadmap to be achieved within the next five years.

As a leader, sharing your vision is vital to inspire and motivate your team. By empowering them to see the bigger picture, they can transcend limitations and focus on what is possible. Clear and passionate communication of the vision fuels energy, purpose and alignment towards common goals.

It's important to create an inclusive environment where everyone feels valued and can contribute their expertise to shape the vision's outcome. When people feel connected to the vision, they become dedicated and committed to its achievement.

Here are some tips to craft a winning professional vision:

▲ Dream big without getting caught up in the details of 'how' it will be accomplished.
▲ Seek inspiration by stepping out of the office and immersing yourself in creative environments.
▲ Disconnect from technology to maintain complete focus on the vision.
▲ Embrace discomfort and think outside the box to unleash creativity.
▲ Learn from the past, address the present and envision the future.

By following these tips and creating a compelling vision, you can inspire your team to reach new heights and drive collective success.

A high-performance vision captures the true spirit and aspirations of the team and shows the legacy that everyone will be proud of being a part of.

Five top tips for creating your personal and professional vision

1. **Be realistic:** Set a vision that is challenging yet achievable.
2. **Communicate:** Share your vision clearly and consistently with others.
3. **Align:** Ensure your vision aligns with your values and strengths.
4. **Be flexible:** Remain open to adjustments and new opportunities.
5. **Take action:** Break down your vision into actionable steps and actively work towards it.

Creating a five-year personal and professional vision provides a sense of direction and purpose, and will allow you to set meaningful goals and make intentional decisions that align with your desired future. This clarity instils confidence and motivation, as it taps into our innate human need for growth, progress and the pursuit of a fulfilling life, propelling us forward with enthusiasm and a sense of accomplishment.

Shannah: I have been making vision boards since I was about twenty years old. It is so nourishing to look back on them and see what my dreams and goals were and where I am at now.

Every two to three years I have updated my vision board and watched it unfold to what it is today, which includes global dreams, big stage speaking engagements, and still supporting individual high performers and all humans who want fresh clarity, purpose and direction with their life plans. My current vision board has the car I want (which I now have), what retirement would look like, all the bucket list travel destinations that excite me, the walking of the world on tracks taken by pilgrims hundreds of years ago, the inspiration of those doing weights and yoga to ensure I age with energy and in the best shape I can be. It has words that truly excite me and keep me on track such as 'where your focus goes your energy flows' and 'you've got this', 'your health is your wealth' and 'control the controllable'.

I get such inspiration each day to make the choices that bring me closer to the vision boards. I spend a lot of time planning, setting goals and fine-tuning my habits for success.

Vision summary

1. The best day of your life is the day you decide to live it.
2. Creating a five-year vision will give your mind a roadmap to follow.
3. Crafting a compelling and exciting vision board brings your dreams to life.
4. Regularly visualising yourself achieving success and incorporating consistent high-performance habits into your routine will align your actions and mindset with your desired outcomes.
5. A powerful professional vision is crucial for guiding teams to new levels of thinking and action.

Create Your Personal High-Performance Plan: VISION

Write out your vision:

_____

_____

_____

To elevate your vision:

What do you need to STOP doing?

1. _____

_____

2. _____

_____

3. _____

_____

What do you need to START doing?

1. _____

_____

2. _____

_____

3. _____

_____

What do you need to KEEP doing?

1. _____

_____

2. _____

_____

3. _____

_____

Chapter 4

Transform Your Mindset

Once your mindset changes, everything on the outside will change along with it

STEVE MARABOLI

How do you achieve more? Live with passion and purpose? Be your authentic self and show up as the best version of you?

There is no one right way, no magic solution, no secret hack. However, there is one thing the most exceptional thinkers and achievers have in common: the *way* they use their mind to *unlock their full potential and live a life of high performance and excellence.*

It's their mindset.

A high-performance mindset involves mental training for increasing competence, self-awareness and self-improvement. It is a series of self-perceptions, attitudes and beliefs people hold about themselves and these determine their behaviour, approach, outlook and mental attitude, and act as a lens through which they see the world.

A high-performance mindset is available to everyone. It's about the ability to create the most optimised inner thoughts, choices and actions for an extraordinary you. Your intentional thoughts are the foundation of a high-performance mindset. How you see yourself, perceive yourself and speak to yourself matters. Consistent and repeated thoughts form patterns that, over time, influence how you see the world; how you view yourself, your potential and your capabilities; and how you approach challenges, setbacks, accomplishment, adversity, failure and successes.

A high-performance mindset is one that has been sharpened by you, is authentic to you and one that only you can create. You can be the driver or the passenger in the mind – it is up to you.

> The only limits to a high-performance mindset, progress, growth and success are the ones that you create.

Many high performers study the work of Stanford University psychologist, Carol Dweck. Dweck researched the concept that there are generally two types of mindsets: a fixed mindset or a growth mindset:

▲ A **fixed** mindset assumes that our character, intelligence and abilities are set and can't be changed in any meaningful way.

▲ A **growth** mindset sees our skills, qualities and intelligence as things that can be improved with effort and persistence, and sees failure as an opportunity for growth and development.

These two mindsets manifest from a very early age and influence your behaviour in both your personal and professional life, and ultimately your capacity to experience happiness, fulfilment and success.

> Our studies show that teaching people to have a growth mindset, which encourages a focus on effort rather than intelligence or talent, helps them to become high achievers in school and life.
>
> – Carol Dweck

Embracing a growth mindset means you believe your skills and intelligence can flourish through dedication and effort. Unlike a fixed mindset, which views abilities as static, a growth mindset fuels the conviction that continuous improvement is possible. Research shows that cultivating a growth mindset fosters tenacity and an unwavering work ethic in individuals of all walks of life.

By embracing the power of a growth mindset, you open the door to boundless possibilities, expanding your horizons and propelling yourself towards a life enriched by continuous growth and happiness.

Is Your Mindset Holding You Back?

Did you know that, on an average day, our minds are filled with approximately 60,000 thoughts? It's astonishing to consider that 80 per cent of these thoughts tend to be negative, and a staggering 95 per cent are repetitive, mirroring the patterns of the previous day. For a long time, it was believed that the brain was fixed, leaving us bound by what we were born with. However, revolutionary research on neuroplasticity has shattered this notion. Neuroplasticity reveals that our brains possess the incredible capacity to rewire themselves, creating new pathways and transforming our thinking patterns. This new-found understanding empowers us to take action and actively train our brains towards a more positive and growth-orientated mindset.

Understanding and acknowledging your current mindset is the first step towards growth and transformation. Only when we consciously decide the kind of mindset we desire can we begin to take action, moving steadfastly towards that mindset and embracing it fully in our daily lives.

Take a look at the table below. What kind of mindset do you believe you possess? Where do you sit on the scale between these two mindsets? Furthermore, consider where you would like to be.

FIXED MINDSET People with this mindset tend to:	GROWTH MINDSET People with this mindset tend to:
Avoid challenges	Embrace challenges
Give up easily	Persist despite setbacks
Respond badly to criticism	Learn from feedback
Feel threatened by talents of others	Be inspired by the success of others
Think effort is unnecessary	Have a strong work ethic
Feel I cannot do it	I can learn new skills
I can't change	I am constantly evolving
If I don't try then I can't fail	I only fail when I stop trying
That job is out of my league	That role looks challenging, I'll apply
This can lead to underperfomance and an unwillingness to learn new things	*This can lead to high achievement and confidence*

Training your mind takes effort, commitment and persistence, just like going to the gym. You don't go to the gym once and think you will be fit forever. Just like you don't do one mind-training activity and think that you will have positive, calm and confident thoughts forever. It requires conscious effort and habit to live this way; however, the benefits far outweigh the effort and upgrade your life in ways you've possibly never dreamt of.

By taking control of your thoughts, you start to focus your attention on what thoughts elevate you and what thoughts drain you. Which ones make you feel awesome and which ones shut you down. Remember back to a time when you felt like you were thriving, unstoppable and at the top of the pyramid. What were your thoughts? What was your energy like? Were you feeling confident? Did your thoughts spur you on? Did they accelerate your experience?

Your time is now, time to elevate, time to upgrade, time to escalate your mindset! It's time to release all the excuses, reasons, rationales and resentments. Today is a fresh canvas, a new day and a new beginning. Your opportunity to step into your growth mindset starts here.

High-performing individuals know the importance of having a positive mindset to achieve high-performance results. The same applies for your everyday life and leadership. You can live in a mindset of fear, stress and worry or you can choose to live in a mindset of clarity, progress and mastery.

Take this opportunity to reflect and envision the mindset that resonates with your aspirations, and let it guide you on the path of personal and professional development. Having a positive mindset is a way of life and is in your control.

The benefits of a positive mindset

A positive mindset has transformative effects on every facet of your life, including your mental well-being, physical health, relationships and career. It empowers you to navigate challenges with resilience and optimism, fosters empathy, enables you to communicate effectively and nurtures deeper connections. Furthermore, it fuels personal growth, enhances productivity and opens doors to new opportunities in your life and career. By adopting a positive mindset, you unlock the extraordinary benefits that can elevate and enrich your entire life:

▲ Longer and healthier life.
▲ Reduced risk of depression.
▲ Lower risk of cardiovascular disease.
▲ Better coping skills during stress.
▲ Enhanced communication.
▲ Improved relationships.
▲ Increased happiness and fulfilment.
▲ Heightened sense of purpose.

Twenty Power Moves to Elevate Your Mindset

Embrace a proactive mindset

To adopt a proactive mindset, it's important to actively shape your thoughts and behaviours. Start by cultivating self-awareness and paying attention to your patterns of thinking and reacting. Take note of any negative or limiting beliefs that may hold you back and consciously work on replacing them with positive and empowering thoughts. Let go of worries about things beyond your control and redirect your energy towards areas where you can make a difference and reframe challenges as opportunities for growth and learning.

Through this proactive approach, you can foster a mindset focused on continuous growth and resilience, and gain a sense of control over your thoughts, actions and responses.

Curate a positive inner circle

Surrounding yourself with positive influences is vital for cultivating a positive mindset. Choose to be around individuals who inspire and encourage personal growth. Engage in supportive communities that foster a positive atmosphere. Limit exposure to negativity and seek out role models who embody the mindset you aspire to have. Be a positive influence yourself by sharing your journey and uplifting others.

By intentionally surrounding yourself with positivity, you create an environment that nurtures personal growth and fosters a positive outlook on life.

Cultivate positive self-talk

Positive self-talk is a powerful practice for reshaping your mindset and promoting personal growth. Try the following tips to flip the switch on negative internal chatter:

- ▲ Challenge and reframe negative thoughts.
- ▲ Replace self-criticism with affirming and empowering statements.
- ▲ Be kind and encouraging to yourself, celebrating achievements and practising self-compassion.
- ▲ Surround yourself with positive influences.
- ▲ Cultivate gratitude.
- ▲ Seek professional help if needed.

Discover the power of helping others

Helping others brings positive changes to social interaction, self-esteem and competence. Extend compassion and kindness by actively listening, lending a hand and performing random acts of kindness (see box below). Volunteer your time and skills to make a difference. Practise empathy and understand others' experiences. Share your knowledge and mentor others.

By helping others, you benefit yourself and create a ripple of positivity.

Random acts of kindness

Random acts of kindness are spontaneous, selfless gestures that bring joy and support to others without expecting anything in return. It's being kind for the sake of being kind. It is giving your best self to others without requests or a promise of return on investment, time or energy. It is simply doing something nice for someone else.

Find your balance

Achieving balance in life is crucial for overall well-being and success. It is important to manage your time effectively by setting clear priorities and organising tasks based on what truly matters to you. You must also establish boundaries to protect your time and energy and get comfortable with saying 'no' to activities that don't align with your priorities (see page 273 for more on this). Prioritising self-care is also critical to achieving balance by taking care of your physical, mental and emotional well-being. Engage in activities that recharge and rejuvenate you.

Empower your life with gratitude

Incorporating gratitude into your daily life can bring about positive changes. Start by taking a moment each day to reflect on the things you're grateful for – it could be the simple joys, supportive relationships or personal achievements. In challenging situations, consciously seeking silver linings or lessons to be learnt and focusing on the positive aspects of your life help foster an attitude of abundance.

By practising gratitude regularly, you can increase happiness, strengthen relationships and cultivate a more positive outlook on life.

Use positive affirmations

Challenge your negative thoughts by incorporating daily positive affirmations. By repeating empowering phrases or statements and truly believing in their truth, you can transform your mindset and bring about a positive shift in your life.

Believe you will succeed

Elevate your life by harnessing the transformative force of self-belief and step into a world of limitless potential. Give yourself the benefit of the doubt and cultivate unwavering confidence in your ability to achieve your goals. With self-belief as your superpower, you open yourself up to boundless possibilities.

By believing in yourself you are recognising your unique talents and embracing your amazing qualities.

Embrace failure

When you embrace failure you gain deeper insight into yourself and learn from your mistakes. Failure is an opportunity to re-evaluate, reflect and discover new ways and strategies to achieve your dreams and goals. By reframing failure as a stepping stone towards success, you can navigate fear with resilience and determination, turning obstacles into opportunities for growth and progress.

Give yourself credit

Give yourself the credit you deserve and elevate your mindset by recognising your own strengths and achievements. Explore how to cultivate self-confidence (see Chapter 6) and celebrate both significant milestones and small victories.

Embrace self-forgiveness

Embracing self-forgiveness can cultivate compassion, kindness and understanding within yourself. By relinquishing self-blame, you embark on a journey of personal growth and inner peace and empower yourself to move forward.

Focus on your health

By placing emphasis on nurturing a healthy body and mind, you will experience a significant boost in energy levels and overall vitality. This upgrade will not only enhance your confidence but also have a transformative impact on every aspect of your life and mindset (see Chapter 6 for more on elevating your health).

Learn new things

When you are learning, you are rewiring your brain, opening yourself up to fresh possibilities and new opportunity, and absorbing new information as you transition into a growth mindset. When you do this you are creating a superior version of yourself.

Take accountability

Taking accountability for your actions leads to much greater self-awareness and helps you to develop a growth mindset where you are always looking to improve and enhance your life. Being accountable will ensure you stay on track with your values, vision and goals.

Create daily habits

Humans are creatures of habit. You are the sum of your habits. Creating routines and positive daily habits that support cognitive function with automation where you don't need to think and remember so much creates a sense of calm, a feeling of control and leads to extraordinary success (see Chapter 12 for more on creating a habit plan).

Step outside your comfort zone

This is where you will elevate into extraordinary growth, transform your mindset and realise that you are truly capable of much more than any limiting beliefs you have created.

Practise patience

Patience helps you to develop a healthy attitude, persevere in the face of setbacks and make more constructive decisions, which often leads to better outcomes.

Ask for help

Life is a constant learning journey. Everyone, including yourself, makes mistakes and needs help and support from others at different times. Don't be too proud to ask for help and support.

Just be yourself

Learning how to be yourself and embrace your own unique qualities can lead to greater self-awareness and appreciation of what you bring to this world. There is only one of you. You are special.

Take action

Taking action is the catalyst that propels you towards your true potential and shapes your destiny. By turning your aspirations into deliberate action, breaking them down into manageable tasks and consistently practising empowering habits, you lay the foundation for success.

Stay committed to taking intentional steps forward in the pursuit of your dreams.

The time to transform and supercharge into a high-performance mindset is now! It's time to step outside your comfort zone and stretch yourself beyond where you ever thought you could go. When you think you can, you can. You can have all the gifts and resources in life, but when you include a supercharged mind, passion, effort, consistency, persistence, courage, humour, intention and taking action as a part of your everyday life, you will elevate and transform your life to achieve greatness.

> Progress is progress, so take small actions towards your goals every day.

A positive mindset will supercharge your life. It will help your overall physical and emotional health, improve your outlook on life, build better coping skills and create longevity.

Shannah: Some gifted athletes rely on their natural ability, but champions know that a major factor in achieving their goals of being the best lies within their powerful mind. They can flip the switch, ignite and perform at their absolute best against the toughest of competition. It is beautiful to watch and I always take those moments, use them for inspiration and apply that energy to my own life. Learning from them, using them as role models, has inspired me to keep sharpening my own mind. How did they talk to themselves, get their grit on, find their purpose and own it? How can I learn from them and fine-tune my attitude, my mindset, my self-talk, even though I am not an athlete (far from it)?

Over the years I have embraced learning the twenty ways to upgrade my mind. From working in a stockbroking firm at eighteen years old with no prior experience, to working in sports management with no prior experience, to being a sponsorship manager to over one hundred athletes, to burnout, to studying coaching twenty years ago when no one knew what it really was, to building the business I wanted that would allow me to safeguard my compromised health and raise a family, positive self-talk has been front and centre.

I am not the fittest, fastest, smartest or happiest person on earth, but I get up each day with an 'I can' attitude and bring it with me all day, working to silence the natural inner critic. I have words on the mirror to train my brain with the words I need for the 'I can' attitude, I have framed prints on the wall with the words and pictures that push me forward, I have my role models' faces on a small board to look at and tap into their mindset, I have a screen saver that elevates me by just looking at it. 'I am inspired. I get to live today. I love myself, I love my life and you've got this' have been trained into my brain on a daily basis to transform my energy and experience of daily life. I have been obsessed with the process as the result is transformational.

Train your mind like you train your body. Take massive action. Be obsessed. I watch my clients transform their lives with fresh clarity, direction and purpose as they retrain their brain with upgraded, powerful, positive and inspirational words. It is pure magic.

Mindset summary

1. A positive mindset is essential for healthy self-esteem.
2. People with a positive mindset often have more confidence, live longer and have a happier relationship with themselves and others.
3. A fixed mindset assumes that our character, intelligence and abilities are set and can't be changed in any meaningful way.
4. A growth mindset sees our skills, qualities and intelligence as things that can be improved with effort and persistence, and sees failure as an opportunity for growth and development.
5. With effort and conviction you can retrain and fully upgrade your thoughts for a high-performance positive mindset.

Create Your Personal High-Performance Plan: MINDSET

Reflect on your current mindset. Is it moving you closer to your vision? If not, define your desired high-performance mindset:

_____

_____

_____

To elevate your mindset:

What do you need to STOP doing?

1. _____

_____

2. _____

_____

3. _____

_____

What do you need to START doing?

1. _____

_____

2. _____

_____

3. _____

_____

What do you need to KEEP doing?

1. _____

_____

2. _____

_____

3. _____

_____

Chapter 5

Reset Your Health

The first wealth is health

RALPH WALDO EMERSON

Your health is your wealth; however, your health is not just whether or not you feel good today. It is a wonderful holistic system with interconnected elements.

Your body, mind, heart and soul are your most valuable possessions. To fully restore, elevate, energise and master your health, it is essential to get in touch with these four main pillars and create actions to amplify your energy:

Physical Health	Mental Health	Emotional Health	Spiritual Health
Energised	Focused	Connected	Aligned
Exercise	Mindfulness	Relationships	Meditation
Nutrition	Learning	Self-awareness	Purpose
Sleep	Stress	Joy	Values
Vitality	Positive	Fulfilment	Reflection

Choosing to focus on your health, remembering that we all have a unique health make-up, so it will look and feel different for everyone, is one of the most empowering and rewarding decisions you can make every day of your life. It will radically transform the levels of vitality and happiness that you experience on a daily basis as you make conscious, committed and long-term small changes for high impact.

When you are physically and mentally strong – whatever that may look like for you – you are more optimistic, motivated, resourceful, tenacious and inspired to keep growing and evolving. Your self-confidence and inner strength is able to deal with what life has in store for you when your four pillars of health are nurtured.

Investing in your health is about embracing a pursuit of growth and unlocking new levels of physical, mental, emotional and spiritual well-being that surpass your expectations. Without staying attuned to your well-being and taking decisive action, your dreams, goals and deepest desires will remain elusive.

You don't need to make big, sweeping changes that you can't stay committed to; this is about making small changes that, over time, will support the four pillars of health, which will in turn support stunning success.

Unlock the actions you need to take to boost your health.

Athletes and high-performing individuals know that their health needs to be a primary focus in all areas to have sustainability over the years. They are committed, put in the work, have a plan, demonstrate discipline, make choices that best serve them and are truly motivated to do what it takes to achieve the goals and dreams they have set.

Choices. We all have them, and it is hard to make great choices in a world of 'instant' – fast food, fast technology, fast consumerism and fast communication. The good news is that making choices for your health to thrive does not require a complex grand plan. It all starts with self-awareness, clarity on where you are at, clarity on how you want to feel and the next choice you make. It is time to elevate.

Take action

▲ How do you want to feel?
▲ Do you want to give to others?
▲ Do you enjoy your family, career, community, hobbies or are you too tired, busy, overwhelmed and disconnected?

Reach further, elevate, rise and aim for your best physically, mentally, emotionally and spiritually.

The Four Pillars of Health

Physical: Your body

Consider:

- ▲ What are you doing for your physical health?
- ▲ Where is the current state of your physical body?
- ▲ How does it feel? Does it give you the energy, vitality and endurance you need to have an awesome day?
- ▲ How would you rate yourself out of 10?

There are so many programs, books and products out there to lose weight, prevent disease and ageing, increase your strength and improve your appearance. The world spends over $100 billion annually searching for a magic solution that will result in the perfect body and flawless external beauty. But there is no easy road or quick fix to your health. Instead, it is about building habits that help and equip you to make healthy and sustainable change, driven with deep purpose.

To enhance your physical health and gain clarity, your purpose – how you want to feel – needs to be defined. What is your long-term purpose? Is it to be strong? Is it to age gracefully? Is it to still be active in your seventies, eighties or nineties? Is it to safeguard against disease? Knowing your purpose, making commitments and taking consistent small actions will result in you experiencing great energy and finding a renewed sense of joy, excitement, motivation and inspiration throughout the different ages and stages of your life.

Take action

▲ What's your purpose?
▲ How do you want to feel?

Hydrate: Embrace the gentle power of water

When it comes to physical health, the focus is usually on eating well, exercising daily and getting enough sleep. While it's important to have these basics in hand – and we'll cover them in detail in Chapter 17 when we home in on the importance of self-care – we also need to focus on hydration when it comes to taking charge of your health as it is an essential component to support your well-being. Water regulates body temperature, lubricates joints, delivers nutrients and keeps organs functioning. Staying hydrated throughout the day by drinking water between meals is important to maintain overall hydration levels. Find your own hydration needs: keep a water bottle with you, set reminders and monitor your caffeine/alcohol intake. Dehydration can be mistaken for a headache or hunger. For optimal hydration, a simple formula is: weight (in kg) multiplied by 0.033.

Note: While it is generally recommended to drink water before or after meals, it is advised to avoid drinking water during meals. This is because consuming water with your meals can dilute digestive juices and enzymes in the stomach, which may hinder the process of proper digestion.

On the following page are some simple ways in which you can prioritise your physical health:

▲ Eliminate or reduce processed foods and replace them with fresh fruit and vegetables.

▲ Eat whole foods where you can.

▲ Use a journal or app to track your meals.

▲ Set aside time each week to plan and prep your meals.

▲ Consider taking supplements.

▲ Establish a consistent sleep schedule and aim for eight hours of sleep per night.

▲ Create a peaceful sleep environment with no tech.

▲ Try to engage in thirty minutes of physical activity per day.

▲ Minimise your caffeine and alcohol intake.

▲ Monitor and maintain your hydration levels during the day.

Take action

Looking at the list above, can you unlock some small actions that will enable you to really take charge of your physical health, right here, right now?

▲ How can you improve your approach to nutrition and enhance your well-being?

▲ What small changes can you make to improve your current movement habits?

▲ Are there any habits or patterns affecting your sleep quality that you can address?

▲ What can you do to better recognise your body's thirst signals and avoid confusing them with hunger?

▲ How can you establish mindful hydration habits that you can consistently follow?

Mental: Your mind

Consider:

- ▲ What are you doing to support your mental health consciously and habitually as part of your daily rituals?
- ▲ Do you feel motivated and inspired in life?
- ▲ Do you feel positive and in control?
- ▲ How would you rate yourself out of 10?

Elevating your mental health refers to focusing on your social and psychological state. Your mental health is shaped by a wide range of varying factors, from genetics, family history and brain chemistry to your personal lifestyle and life experiences. You can work on your mental health by learning how to manage excess stress, worry and anxiety.

Mental factors such as self-belief and confidence are essential for performance and can take your life to a whole new level. In the practice of positive psychology there are three important skills to master to fine-tune your mental health:

1. **Learn from the past:** Reflect on previous experiences, identify lessons learnt and apply those insights to make informed decisions and avoid repeating past mistakes.
2. **Live in the present:** Engage fully in the present moment, embracing the here and now with mindfulness and awareness. Focus on the task at hand, savour the simple joys and appreciate the beauty that surrounds you.
3. **Plan for the future:** Set clear goals and establish a strategic roadmap to achieve them. Break down long-term aspirations into actionable steps, create a timeline and stay committed to making progress towards your desired future outcomes.

Self-awareness and knowledge are the keys to assessing your mental health. When you know your strengths, values, purpose and interests, you can express your best self, commit to mental health practices to sharpen the mind to make good career, relationship and life choices, and handle events and emotions with perspective. Paying attention to your own mental state gives you an insight into recognising your emotions, thoughts and physical state, such as fatigue or overwhelm, and will give you clues as to when you need to support them.

There are many high-performance tools, tips and techniques available for mental health that can be incorporated into our routines and rituals to support the mind, but we see visualisation, positive self-talk, managing your time and being open to a growth mindset as the basics to master.

Visualisation

Mental training helps you perform at your best, both mentally and physically. As we've explored, visualisation is a powerful technique to master and to elevate and escalate your commitment to health (see page 68). Imagine yourself feeling strong, flexible, at the top of your game and full of vitality. What does it feel like? Use this to build confidence, enhance performance, decrease anxiety, reduce pain, adopt better behaviours and make better choices for your body each day. Listen to a guided meditation, create a vision board, use flash cards and design your screen saver with uplifting quotes, beautiful landscapes and images of loved ones, creating a visual reminder that inspires and motivates you every time you glance at your screen. Visualisations and mental imagery impact your articulation, planning and memory. Training your brain helps boost motivation and improves performance.

Positive self-talk

Positive self-talk is the opposite of the inner critic. It's an internal monologue that helps you feel better about yourself, to be more optimistic and resilient, and that encourages you to keep going when the results are slower than you would like.

Recognising and overcoming our inner critic is essential for personal growth and well-being. The inner critic – that nagging voice within – often undermines our confidence, amplifies self-doubt and hinders progress. To conquer this, we must first cultivate self-awareness to identify its presence and patterns. By questioning the validity of its negative thoughts and reframing them with self-compassion and positivity, we can challenge and gradually diminish its influence. Embracing self-acceptance, practising self-care and seeking support from others can also aid in silencing the inner critic, empowering us to embrace our true potential and live a more fulfilling life.

To improve your self-esteem, stress management and reduce symptoms of anxiety, overwhelm and depression, your words really matter. They are powerful. It takes your mind from 'I don't know anything' to 'I want to learn'. It takes you from 'I can't do it' to 'I will give it my best shot'. Ultimately when you change your words you can change your life. Affirmations are a power tool, training the brain with 'I am' and 'I can' statements, such as: 'I can do this', 'I am strong', 'I can say no'.

Mirror work

Mirror work refers to a practice of self-reflection and self-acceptance that involves looking into a mirror and engaging in positive affirmations, self-talk or self-examination. It is a powerful technique used to develop self-awareness, build self-esteem and foster a deeper connection with oneself. Mirror work often involves speaking affirmations or positive statements aloud while looking directly into your own eyes in the mirror, reinforcing self-love, self-compassion and self-acceptance. By facing and addressing your inner thoughts, beliefs and emotions through the mirror, you can cultivate a greater sense of self-empowerment and personal growth. Mirror work can be a transformative tool for enhancing self-confidence, self-image and self-worth.

Time management

Time management is really 'personal management' and is a skill to put some laser focus on to achieve an optimal quality of life with outstanding results. Elite time management safeguards performance, achievement, job satisfaction and overall well-being while lowering stress. Own your time. We all have twenty-four hours a day. Use your minutes carefully.

To optimise time management, it's important to shift our focus from multitasking to task batching. Multitasking – attempting to handle multiple tasks simultaneously – can reduce focus and efficiency. Instead, task batching involves grouping similar activities together and allocating dedicated time blocks for specific tasks to maximise productivity. By batching similar tasks together, such as replying to emails, making phone calls or working on creative projects, you can minimise context-switching and increase efficiency.

This approach also allows you to streamline your workflow, maintain focus, reduce distractions and make better use of your time and energy. By adopting task batching, we can enhance our ability to manage time effectively, achieve a better balance in our personal and professional lives, and improve overall productivity.

Growth mindset

As we explored in the last chapter, the mindset you have directs your thoughts, emotions and ultimately actions to either success or failure. Your mind is your most potent ally towards mitigating disease and manifesting daily vitality and great energy. A growth mindset gives you the resilience to learn from both failures and success, and is a strong component of mental health training. Your mindset can have a profound effect on your physical health and your emotional well-being. Challenge yourself to elevate with an open mind, strong situational awareness and pledge to take responsibility for controlling the controllable.

Below are some simple ways in which you can elevate your mental health:

▲ Practise guided meditation.
▲ Prioritise self-care and make it a non-negotiable part of your routine.
▲ Engage in regular exercise.
▲ Take breaks and allow yourself moments of rest and relaxation.
▲ Prioritise quality sleep to recharge and rejuvenate.
▲ Find hobbies and activities that bring you fulfilment.
▲ Create a music playlist that elevates your mood.
▲ Set boundaries and learn to say no to protect your mental well-being.

▲ Use empowering 'I am', 'I can' statements.

▲ Focus on solutions rather than dwelling on the problems.

Take action

▲ What resonated with you in the list above?

▲ What can you stop, start and keep when it comes to your mental health?

▲ How can you elevate?

Emotional: Your heart

Consider:

▲ What is the current state of your emotional health?

▲ Do you feel like your cup is full?

▲ Are you open to receiving?

▲ Have you enough to give?

▲ How would you rate yourself out of 10?

Emotional health is about how you feel and refers to your ability to cope with both positive and negative emotions and accept and manage feelings through challenges and change. Emotional health includes both emotional intelligence and emotional regulation. Like ocean waves, our days come in highs and lows, ebbing and flowing and constantly changing. Focusing on elevating your emotional health will lead to resilience and self-awareness so you can ride the waves and feelings without being thrown off course by a big emotionally disruptive tidal wave.

We see examples of strong emotional health when we watch sport and see athletes handle winning and losing and everything in between.

Emotional health matters to all ages, all over the world. Being human means facing challenges. We all have 'suffering' in common. We will all face adversity in our lifetime, so getting clear and understanding how you express your emotions, knowing who supports you emotionally and how you will cope when times get tough is worth spending some time on.

In our journey to enhance emotional health, there are several tools we can incorporate. Mindfulness practices such as meditation can help us stay present, cultivate self-awareness and manage emotions effectively. Journaling (see box below) allows us to express and process our feelings, gaining clarity and insights into our emotional landscape. Seeking support from therapists or counsellors can provide valuable guidance and tools to navigate emotional challenges. Additionally, building a strong social support network of friends and loved ones who provide understanding, empathy and encouragement can contribute significantly to our emotional well-being. Remember, these tools serve as valuable resources on our path to nurturing and elevating our emotional health.

The power of journaling

Journaling is a personal practice of writing down thoughts, emotions and experiences in a dedicated journal. It offers the benefits of self-reflection, self-expression and gaining insights into one's own thoughts and feelings, promoting emotional clarity, self-discovery and personal growth.

Self-confidence

Self-confidence is built upon choices, small wins and accomplishments that ignite passion and bring happiness and pride. It involves finishing tasks, following values, mastering strengths, exercising, taking calculated risks and focusing on long-term happiness. To become emotionally fit, calm and confident, several tools can be incorporated into our journey:

▲ Self-reflection through journaling or introspection helps us gain insights into our strengths, areas of growth and values.
▲ Developing emotional regulation skills, such as deep-breathing techniques or mindfulness practices, allows us to manage and navigate challenging emotions effectively.
▲ Practising self-compassion and cultivating a positive mindset helps foster resilience and self-acceptance.
▲ Seeking personal growth opportunities through workshops, courses or reading can expand our knowledge and skills, boosting confidence in various areas of life.
▲ Building a strong support network of mentors, friends or support groups provides encouragement, feedback and guidance as we navigate our path towards self-confidence.

The journey to self-confidence is lifelong.

Self-regulation

Self-regulation requires self-awareness and monitoring of your emotional state and responses to situations and events. To upgrade your self-regulation, create mental space with a big breath. As emotions happen quickly, we need time to respond rather than hastily react. Oxygen is picked up by the blood's haemoglobin and transported to the body's cells, where it is used to release energy and calm your emotions. For peak oxygenation of the body, high performers learn to master breathing. Take a breath. Notice what you feel, name what you feel, accept the emotion, identify and reduce your triggers and consider the story you are telling yourself. Your words matter.

Imagine you're in a challenging meeting at work or discussion at home with your partner, children or friends where tensions are rising. As the conversation intensifies, you feel your heart racing, your muscles tensing and frustration mounting. In that moment, you take a deep breath, allowing oxygen to flow through your body, bringing a sense of calm. You pause and observe the emotions bubbling up within you, acknowledging that you're feeling overwhelmed and irritated. By naming and accepting these emotions without judgement, you create space for a more intentional response. Recognising that the triggering factors may be certain behaviours or comments, you consciously choose not to engage in a reactive manner.

Instead, you remind yourself of the story you want to tell yourself – the narrative of composure, professionalism and effective communication. With a calmer demeanour and a clear mind, you navigate the meeting or discussion assertively, expressing your thoughts and concerns while maintaining emotional balance. In this example, the conscious practice of self-regulation through breathing, self-awareness and intentional response helps you navigate challenging situations with poise and clarity.

Inner harmony

Inner well-being comes from the connection and harmony between our inner life and the outside world. Inner harmony is a peace of mind that springs from acceptance of ourselves, of others, of our circumstances and of the past. Practising activities that bring you peace and allow the calm to come, such as taking a bath, conscious breathwork, laughing, pausing, taking a break from technology, having a massage, walking in nature and listening to music all add to your level and stability of strong emotional health.

Relationships

Emotionally healthy relationships are essential for your overall well-being. To improve how you show up in your relationships, start by staying present. Dedicate your full attention by actively listening (see box on the following page) and engaging in meaningful conversations. Set personal goals that align with your growth and share them with others, encouraging mutual support and shared aspirations.

Invite open communication by creating a safe and non-judgemental space for honest expression. Relationships require effort, so be willing to invest time, energy and effort into nurturing and strengthening them.

Reflect on your interactions, learn from past experiences and embrace self-reflection as it provides an opportunity for growth and personal development, allowing you to foster healthier and more fulfilling connections with others.

How to be a great listener

The power of becoming a great listener lies in the ability to truly understand others, foster deeper connections and create an environment of trust and empathy. When people actively listen to one another, it enables effective communication, builds trust and encourages engagement. It also promotes empathy and understanding.

Supporting emotional health through becoming a great listener involves offering a safe and non-judgemental space for others to express their emotions. By actively listening and showing genuine empathy, you validate their experiences and provide emotional support. Engaging in reflective listening, asking open-ended questions and offering comforting words can help individuals feel heard, understood and less alone in their struggles. Being a great listener allows you to cultivate stronger relationships, deepen connections and contribute to the emotional well-being of others, which in turn can positively impact your own emotional health.

Below are some simple ideas to help you elevate your emotional health:

- ▲ Express what you are good at.
- ▲ Challenge yourself to try new things.
- ▲ Keep a journal to monitor your emotions.
- ▲ Do ten minutes of conscious breathwork.
- ▲ Walk in nature.
- ▲ Create some tech-free time.
- ▲ Be present when others are speaking.
- ▲ Respect other people's emotions.

▲ Admit when you are wrong.
▲ Show respect during conflict.

Take action

▲ Are there some small steps from the list above that you can take today?
▲ What can you stop, start and keep?
▲ How can you elevate?

Spiritual: Your soul

Consider:

▲ What are you doing for your spiritual health?
▲ Do you feel present?
▲ Do you feel part of something bigger than yourself?
▲ Do you feel there is meaning in your life?
▲ How would you rate yourself out of 10?

At its core, spirituality represents a profound and personal connection to something greater than oneself. It encompasses a holistic approach to life, integrating the physical, psychological and social dimensions of human existence. Spiritual well-being involves finding meaning and purpose, fostering a sense of belonging and aligning with one's beliefs, values and ethics. It is a journey of self-discovery and growth that brings depth, fulfilment and a profound connection to the world around us.

Working on and elevating your spiritual health will enhance the quality of your life and your sense of purpose and meaning.

It can include your beliefs, culture, community, values, codes of conduct and the personal ethics you hold dear.

When you are spiritually healthy you will feel more connected not only to a higher purpose and power, but to others around you. You will have clarity when it comes to making everyday choices and your actions will be in alignment with your beliefs and values. It promotes a higher and more elevated feeling of purpose, hope, peace and meaning.

When you grow spiritually, you elevate to a level where you can have compassion, empathy, kindness and understanding of others. You can reflect on the meaning of events, deal with life's ups and downs and bounce back from difficult situations and experiences. Spiritual strength is needed to overcome hardships, meet challenges and continue with a purposeful life.

Service to others

When giving to others, whether it be time, food, clothing, money, shelter or your expertise, happiness rebounds like a boomerang that strikes you in the heart and fills your own tank. Giving when the recipients are grateful elevates your own self-esteem and fuels your self-confidence. Thinking and speaking well of others is the basis of generous giving.

Neurochemicals of happiness exist within the brain and include dopamine, serotonin and oxytocin. Being of service to others, lifting others and supporting others releases these feel-good hormones, filling your happiness tank, promoting a sense of euphoria and calming your mind and body. The old adage, 'It is better to give than to receive' has never been truer. How do you give? When you have in the past how did it feel?

Mindfulness

Mindfulness is the simplest, clearest, purest train of thought you can have. It is a form of meditation. Mindfulness can be a highly effective tool for your spiritual growth and development. Mindfulness is paying deliberate and non-judgemental attention to the present moment. You are connected to the moment. It is an approach of open awareness and is practised and mastered by high performers and athletes to regulate their bodies and minds at the peak of performance.

Become a master of open awareness by focusing on your breath to bring you into the present moment – tasting your food, feeling the sun on your skin, noticing the birds, listening to music with no distraction, feeling the water while showering, smelling the roses. Tapping into your five senses, you will find a gateway to the present moment and enhance your spiritual health. This can be practised at any time, right now: wake up, take a look – there is magic everywhere around you.

Gratitude

Embracing gratitude as a spiritual practice is the key to having a full heart. It involves feeling and expressing appreciation for the people and things in our lives, as well as the natural world around us. It allows you to cherish, savour and have pure self-awareness in the present moment in ways that make you feel abundant. Writing in a gratitude journal is a high-performance practice to elevate your spiritual life.

Writing daily expressions of gratitude, embracing present experiences and appreciating those in our lives deepens our sense of belonging on earth and spiritually empowers us to cultivate a profound connection and purpose in our existence.

Become a master of being thankful for the pleasing things that happen to you and that you experience in life, no matter how big or small. It all adds deep and soul-nourishing fulfilment to your daily life.

Integrity

Authenticity and being a person of your word allows you to connect to others with more depth. It commands the discipline of self-reflection, self-awareness and an uncompromising willingness to be brutally honest with yourself. Integrity is defined as moral soundness, genuineness and wholeness, and is represented in your beliefs and the way you think, speak and act, especially when no one is watching. Practising the art of honesty, respect, keeping promises, taking responsibility and generating trust are the foundations of spiritual integrity. How have you felt being around someone with a lack of integrity? How did it make you feel?

Take a look at the list below of some simple steps you can take to elevate your spiritual health:

> The golden rule of integrity is 'do unto others as you would have them do to you'.

- ▲ Let others know you love them.
- ▲ Do what you say you will do.
- ▲ Offer to help others.
- ▲ Notice and admire nature.
- ▲ Consciously taste your food and drinks.
- ▲ Practise the art of thank you.
- ▲ Follow through on promises.
- ▲ Refrain from sharing others' secrets.
- ▲ Return items you have borrowed.
- ▲ Set a positive example; be a role model for others.

Take action

▲ Take a look at the list on the previous page – what small steps can you take today?

▲ What can you stop, start and keep?

▲ How can you elevate?

When you take full and total ownership of your life, your health and the choices you make, you will feel liberated, empowered and inspired by life itself. To do so you must lift and elevate, and focus on the choices you are making every day and ask yourself whether they work for you. Do they give you the results you want? Do they result in high-performance living?

Reach up, lift higher, fine-tune your habits and routines, and achieve your best peak performance – physically, mentally, emotionally and spiritually – and you will be unstoppable and experience your best life. We only get one life. Let's start with making one choice and commit to it.

Colleen: My value of health is not a sometimes-on proposition – it is always top of mind. I worked out throughout my career that if I wanted to be able to juggle my life, career, be there for my family and friends, my team and give back to the community, I needed to be good to myself, before I could be good to anyone else. I learnt this lesson the hard way . . . when I hit burnout.

For me, physical health is a daily commitment and practice. I walk between 5 and 8 kilometres every day, and when I say every day, I mean it. It doesn't matter if it's raining, if I am tired or if I just can't be bothered – there are no excuses.

Moving my body is the commitment and promise I make to myself and is the first thing I do when I get up. No technology, no emails, no phone calls and no coffee until I have moved my body. It's not just about the benefits walking has on my body, but also my mind.

I start the day with fresh air in my lungs, positive thoughts in my head and a mindset that today is going to be amazing: it will bring new opportunities, I will meet new people and make new memories. I tell myself that, today, I get to live another extraordinary day.

Health summary

1. Taking charge of your health requires focus and self-awareness.
2. Physical health can elevate through the choices of how you eat, move, sleep and hydrate.
3. Mental health can elevate through visualisation, positive self-talk, time management and fostering a growth mindset.
4. Emotional health deepens when we focus on breath, regulation, understanding inner harmony and creating safe relationships.
5. Spiritual health aligns through serving others, practising mindfulness and living in gratitude and with integrity.

Create Your Personal High-Performance Plan: HEALTH

To elevate each pillar of health:

What do you need to STOP doing?

1. Physical health: _____

_____

2. Mental health: _____

_____

3. Emotional health: _____

_____

4. Spiritual health: _____

_____

What do you need to START doing?

1. Physical health: _____

_____

2. Mental health: _____

_____

3. Emotional health: _____

_____

4. Spiritual health: _____

_____

What do you need to KEEP doing?

1. Physical health: _____

_____

2. Mental health: _____

_____

3. Emotional health: _____

_____

4. Spiritual health: _____

_____

Chapter 6

Elevate Your Confidence

The most beautiful thing
you can wear is confidence

BLAKE LIVELY

Have you ever met a person either in a social or professional situation and been in awe of how much confidence they had? Did you then walk away and tell yourself a version of, 'They must have been born confident'; 'I bet they are an extrovert'; 'They are an overachiever'; or 'They must live a perfect life full of success, accomplishment and happiness'?

The truth is none of us are born with confidence. Equally, none of us are immune to confidence issues such as imposter syndrome and self-doubt – and we have both experienced these at different points in our lives. Some of us suffer a little and some a lot, but this lack of confidence shows up in even the most seemingly confident people.

Whether it's walking into a boardroom of strangers and wondering, 'Should I be here? Am I good enough?', doing a presentation and questioning whether the audience were engaged or meeting new people and wondering if they liked you, this lack of confidence goes far and wide. Many people we meet at speaking events, people we coach and people who attend our programs often reveal that they lack confidence and experience self-doubt, either in their personal lives, career, appearance or the way they see themselves compared to others.

Having a lack of confidence can have a dramatic effect on your career and relationships. It prevents you from putting your hand up for promotions, trying new things, speaking your truth and truly valuing yourself. It often keeps you in your safe lane – the one where you feel most comfortable because you fear disappointment and failure. It might be the reason you stay in a toxic relationship or constantly underplay your skills and abilities or don't go after what you really want in life.

When we don't feel confident, it is easy to self-sabotage and compare ourselves to other people's lives and success.

But confidence is vital for high-performance living. It is an overarching attitude and the basis of self-belief and self-worth. It is the characteristic that distinguishes those who do, from those who simply imagine.

Know that it is absolutely possible to make positive changes and cultivate confidence in all areas of your life. It starts with believing in your potential and recognising that change is within your reach. Embrace the idea that personal growth is a continuous journey, and each step forward, no matter how small, contributes to your overall transformation.

Remember, confidence is not a fixed trait but a skill that can be developed over time. Embrace the process, be patient with yourself and celebrate every triumph, no matter how small. Believe in your ability to create positive change and know that a more confident and empowered version of you is waiting to be unleashed. Embrace the possibilities and embark on this transformative journey with courage and determination.

What Is Confidence?

Before exploring the essence of confidence, it is essential to understand what confidence is not:

- ▲ It is not about 'faking it till you make it'.
- ▲ It is not about trying to be someone you are not.
- ▲ It is not about being arrogant or rude.
- ▲ It is not about shifting responsibility.
- ▲ It is not about judging others.
- ▲ It is not about exaggerated conviction.

▲   It is not about thinking you are the smartest person in the room.
▲   It is not about having an over-inflated ego or opinion of yourself.

Instead, confidence revolves around the ability to make smart choices for yourself and believe in your own judgement and capabilities. It involves recognising your worth regardless of imperfections or external opinions. Individuals with confidence typically exhibit a positive mindset (as discussed in Chapter 4), are self-motivated, and confront their failures while drawing lessons from them.

You cultivate a sense of confidence through mastering skills and accomplishing goals. This in turn fosters the belief that with dedicated learning and hard work in specific areas of your life, you can do great things. This kind of confidence helps you face challenges and tough times, work on areas of life where confidence is lacking, and persist in the face of setbacks.

Developing good habits, cultivating positive routines, incorporating structure into your life, celebrating your achievements and envisioning future aspirations will invigorate your confidence and propel your life towards greater fulfilment, happiness and success.

Confident individuals feel comfortable with themselves, which generates trust and encourages others to have confidence in them. However, maintaining self-confidence isn't always easy, especially if you tend to be negative or hard on yourself.

Having self-confidence is critical, but many people struggle with it. Those who lack confidence are less likely to achieve success and do well in life. Those with confidence inspire it in others – their clients, colleagues and family and friends – which in turn boosts their self-assurance and ability to achieve success.

Myths about confidence

There are so many myths about confidence. If we start to believe these myths, we can find ourselves living with self-doubt and self-sabotage. We can even begin to feel that confidence is out of reach for us.

> Every day is a new day and another opportunity to enhance your confidence and live a life of self-mastery, purpose and passion.

Here are some of the biggest confidence myths we have encountered or experienced throughout our lives and careers. It's time to squash these misconceptions and allow you to upgrade your confidence inside and out.

Myth 1: You are born with confidence

Nobody is born with confidence; it's something you develop and strive for as you go through life and experience new situations and environments. The good news is that confidence is a skill that can be learnt. Like any new skill, it takes time and effort to grow and nourish it. Confidence is like a muscle – the more you use it the more powerful your confidence becomes. When you confront challenging situations, push yourself outside your comfort zone and do things you never imagined or thought possible, you are supercharging your confidence.

Myth 2: You either have it or you don't

If you are a confident person today or this week, that doesn't necessarily mean this will be the case next week or next month. Confidence shows up at different times throughout your life. When good things happen, such as winning an award, hitting budget or getting a compliment, your confidence rises. When not-so-good things happen, such as missing out on a promotion, receiving a customer complaint or a relationship breakdown, your confidence plummets. When you acknowledge that confidence is situational, you are better equipped to deal with good and bad situations.

Myth 3: Extroverts are more confident

When you think about a confident person, you often picture someone who is highly extroverted. However, extroverts don't necessarily have more confidence than introverts; they are often just louder! Being extroverted or introverted has nothing to do with your confidence, it's all about what energises or drains you. An introvert who has strong values and is self-aware can be just as confident as an extrovert. So, it doesn't matter whether your personality leans more towards introversion or extroversion, you have the ability to build confidence. It takes practice, commitment and persistence.

Myth 4: It must be perfect before I start

Whether applying for a promotion, starting your own business or training for a marathon, many often feel everything needs to be perfect before taking that scary first step. This diminishes your confidence and prevents you from achieving what you set out to do. You need to change the story you are telling yourself. You need to stop striving for perfection as trying to be perfect only ends up in disappointment and self-sabotage, and is one of the biggest confidence killers. Instead, think about moving from perfection to progress, having a go and doing your best.

Myth 5: Only achievement builds confidence

We all want to achieve extraordinary things in life, but we need to remember that building confidence is a daily act and we should acknowledge our small achievements. Often, we neglect these and focus instead on larger goals. By celebrating smaller wins, we train our brains to recognise our progress. When you stop and celebrate your achievements, it not only gives you an awesome rush of dopamine, it also builds your confidence and self-worth, allows you to try new things and gives you the motivation to keep going. A great hair day, committing to your morning routine, finishing a project on time, dropping those couple of kilos, improving on your previous score or speaking up in a meeting are all achievements to celebrate. Focus on the little wins as well as the big ones. They all help to enhance your confidence and self-worth, and validate all the great things you have to offer to the world. Small achievements give you the confidence to build up to extraordinary achievements.

Myth 6: Confident people don't feel insecure or afraid

Confidence does not mean the absence of fear or insecurities. Life throws you many curveballs and challenges, and feeling insecure or afraid is part of being human. Feeling anxious or nervous is a normal reaction to taking risks or trying something new. It could be moving cities, changing jobs, talking to a stranger, jumping out of a plane or trying something new. When doing anything for the first time you are stepping out of your comfort zone and it can feel uncomfortable, and you can feel afraid. Don't stop. Keep going. As Susan Jeffers said, 'Feel the fear and do it anyway'! What you are doing when you try something new is building confidence. Confidence starts with the willingness to **try**. When we **try**, we **build skills**; when we **build skills**, we **build competency**; and when we **build competency**, we **build confidence**.

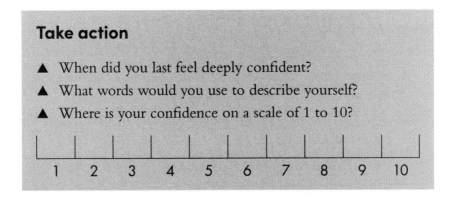

Take action

▲ When did you last feel deeply confident?

▲ What words would you use to describe yourself?

▲ Where is your confidence on a scale of 1 to 10?

1	2	3	4	5	6	7	8	9	10

Overcoming Common Confidence Crushers

What holds you back from elevating your life and living with confidence? Let's look now at some of the common obstacles and how you can overcome them.

Fear of being judged

A lack of confidence often comes from a fear of being judged. It is linked to your natural desire to be liked and prevents you from speaking up, asking for help and sharing your opinions and ideas. This fear, in most cases, reflects your own insecurities. You judge yourself on what you think is acceptable and often when people are judging others it's because they are lacking self-acceptance and love. If you could learn to love yourself more, you would live with more compassion and less judgement.

What you can do

▲ **Know your values and let them be your lighthouse for all your decision-making (see Chapter 2).**

▲ **Be your authentic self and don't try to be anyone else:** There is only ever going to be one of you.

▲ **Never take judgement personally:** You know yourself better than anyone else.

▲ **Take feedback and criticism on board and use it to evolve and grow.**

▲ **Treat yourself with care and respect:** Practise positive self-compassion.

▲ **Stop overthinking:** Constant worrying and overthinking can often diminish your confidence. Believe in yourself and go for it.

Listening to your inner critic

We all have one! Your inner critic often turns up when you are under stress or pressure and the more you entertain your inner critic the stronger it becomes. Your inner critic often says things like: 'I'm going to fail!', 'I am not worthy', 'I am not smart enough', 'I'm underprepared', 'I don't fit in', 'I need more skills' or 'I don't deserve success'. Your inner critic is highly judgemental, can leave you feeling miserable and stuck, sabotage your success and hold you back from excelling in life and experiencing joy.

What you can do

▲ **Pause and reflect:** Are your inner critic's thoughts and judgements based on reality or are they stories you're telling yourself?

▲ **Recognise when your inner critic surfaces and create a more positive and empowering story:** Remind yourself of your strengths and achievements and focus on your potential. Avoid dwelling on your thoughts as this reactivates your inner critic. Instead, shift your focus and move forward.

▲ **Build in a daily practice of gratitude:** This will promote positive self-talk and build confidence (see page 306).

▲ **Build a strong, wise and compassionate voice inside of you:** This will allow you to disarm your inner critic and overcome negative thoughts.

Change your story, change your life

We are constantly creating stories as our minds try to make sense of what's happening around us. We are continually tapping into our past, which shapes our beliefs about who we are, what we believe to be true, what we are capable of and what we think we deserve. The stories we tell ourselves can negatively impact our confidence.

We need to interrupt this story to prevent it from taking control, and create a more empowering story that helps us feel confident to take action.

What stories does your inner critical voice tell you? (Tick the story you use the most.)

O 'I'm destined to fail.'
O 'I'm burdened with guilt.'
O 'I'm constantly under pressure.'
O 'I don't belong or fit in.'
O 'I lack necessary skills.'
O 'I'm not worthy or good enough.'

If any of these resonated with you, here are some practical tips to help transform your narrative and embrace the confidence to take action:

▲ **Challenge beliefs:** Question the validity of negative beliefs and consider if they are based on outdated perceptions. Look for empowering perspectives that uplift you.
▲ **Reframe your narrative:** Take control of your story by focusing on your strengths, achievements and potential. Emphasise resilience and growth instead of dwelling on failures.

▲ **Affirm your capabilities:** Remind yourself of past successes to boost confidence.

▲ **Visualise success:** Use the power of visualisation to imagine yourself confidently taking action and achieving your goals, which can help build confidence and motivation.

Remember, changing your story is a process. Be patient and kind to yourself as you work towards creating a more empowering narrative that fuels your confidence and motivates you to take action.

Lack of self-belief

If you don't believe in yourself, no one else will. The way you perceive yourself, believe in yourself, talk to yourself and think about yourself will also affect the way others see you.

Without the ability to believe in your own worth – which includes believing you are worthy of love, and valuing your own opinions, thoughts and interests – you will be constantly comparing yourself to others and rob yourself of reaching your full potential and living the extraordinary life you deserve.

What you can do

▲ **Be your own supporter:** Believe in yourself and become your own biggest fan. Speak to yourself with kindness and encouragement, just as you would to your best friend.

▲ **Surround yourself with your cheer squad:** People who genuinely care about you and will support you through ups and downs. Their encouragement and belief in you can help bolster your self-belief.

▲ **Guard your well-being:** Minimise your exposure to unsupportive or negative influences. Such influences can erode your self-belief and hinder your confidence and personal growth.

▲ **Avoid comparing yourself to others:** Comparing yourself to others can erode your self-belief. Remember that everyone has their unique journey and strengths. Focus on your own progress and growth.

▲ **Celebrate efforts and accomplishments:** Celebrate these no matter how small. Recognise your progress and achievements along the way. Celebrating builds confidence and motivates you to keep pushing forward.

▲ **Practise gratitude:** Shift your thoughts towards a more positive and empowering mindset of gratitude. Focus on what you have and appreciate your strengths, opportunities and experiences (see page 306).

Fear of embarrassment

Most people are so scared of and uncomfortable about being embarrassed that they'll do almost anything to avoid it. They are afraid that people will think badly of them and judge them, and that they won't measure up in comparison to others. The thought of being embarrassed or humiliated can prevent you from accepting challenges, trying new things, making the most of your opportunities and taking healthy risks. However, there is power in learning to deal with embarrassment, rather than trying to avoid it.

What you can do

▲ **Get comfortable in the uncomfortable:**
Acknowledging and embracing your feelings of
embarrassment is a natural part of the learning process, and
when we embrace discomfort we can use this for a catalyst
for growth. Embracing your feelings of embarrassment
may look like willingly participating in a public
speaking event despite feeling nervous and vulnerable,
as you recognise it as an opportunity to develop your
communication skills and build self-confidence.

▲ **Allow yourself to become more vulnerable:** Don't
be afraid to share your feelings of embarrassment and talk
through what happened with a trusted friend or family
member.

▲ **Practise self-compassion:** We all mess up because we're
human. If you experience an embarrassing moment,
practise compassion towards yourself. Beating yourself up
only puts you in a fixed mindset.

▲ **Own your mistakes:** This shows self-awareness,
authenticity and courage. If you can admit when you
made a mistake this can help you move on.

▲ **Stay calm:** When you are embarrassed, the anxiety can
be overwhelming. Keep calm and rise up. Taking three
deep breaths can help.

▲ **Learn from your embarrassing moments:** Finding
the lesson can help you grow and better prepare for future
situations and gain a sense of control.

Fear of appearing arrogant

Fear of appearing arrogant can prevent you from being more engaged, speaking up in meetings, asking direct questions and putting yourself forward in different situations. However, there is a huge difference between confidence and arrogance. Arrogant people act as if they are superior, more valuable, get lost in their own importance and proceed through life with a sense of entitlement. Confident people believe in themselves and their abilities, feel comfortable in their own skin and know their true worth.

What you can do

▲ **Focus your attention outwards:** Arrogance is inherently self-centred. A confident person spends more time thinking about how other people feel.

▲ **Avoid comparing yourself to others:** The only comparison that matters is the comparison between your present self and the high performer you want to become.

▲ **Collaborate, don't dominate:** When you create an inclusive environment, you energise and cultivate a culture of collaboration that is both productive and joyful.

▲ **Let people speak and don't interrupt:** Interrupting is the exact opposite of listening. You learn and grow when you are listening rather than speaking (see page 165).

▲ **Celebrate and shine light on the success of others:** This inspires others to raise the bar and increases people's sense of well-being. When you enjoy the success of others, you also increase the likelihood of your own success.

▲ **Look for opportunities to compliment people:** Set a goal of saying something nice to someone every day. This will train the brain to think with a more positive mindset and can help to improve other people's opinion of you.

Guilt

Guilt in your life can be debilitating and paralyse you from living with confidence and elevating your life. You will often feel guilty about taking care of yourself and can be reluctant to do anything that might seem self-indulgent or selfish. This is often because you tell yourself that you have other priorities and more important things to do. You can also feel guilty about having said the wrong thing to a friend, for not remembering someone's birthday, because there's nothing in the fridge for dinner or because you mixed up the kids' lunch boxes.

What you can do

- ▲ **Prioritise your own self-care:** As we'll explore further in Chapter 17, self-care is not selfish. It is essential to living life with a full tank. You can only be good to others when you are good to yourself first. You should never feel guilty about making decisions to take care of yourself. Instead, try finding joy and pleasure in everything that you do and build self-care into all aspects of your life. Replace your guilty feelings with positive emotions and raise your confidence.
- ▲ **Appreciate yourself and all that you do:** Write a self-gratitude diary at the end of each day (see page 306) or make a note in your phone to get into the practice of focusing on what you *did* achieve.
- ▲ **Forgive yourself:** A lack of forgiveness can hold you back from living life and building extraordinary confidence. Stop fixating on what you could have done differently and forgive yourself. Let go of guilt and give yourself permission to step into your confident self.

The gender divide

Women seem particularly prone to experiencing self-doubt and lack of confidence which holds them back from unlocking their full potential. The largest global study in 2021 into women's confidence conducted by Women's Confidence found that only 3.4 per cent of women rate their confidence high (9–10).

Women need to be confident in their abilities so that they can achieve the goals and dreams they set for themselves. Once you believe you can, you are more likely to make your goals and dreams a reality.

How to Build Real Confidence

Let's now explore how to build real confidence, believe in yourself and elevate in the three pillars of life, leadership and longevity so that you can live an extraordinary life.

To be confident means living a life of fulfilment, passion and purpose. Building confidence is a work in progress – and no matter how big or small the steps, progress is progress.

Real confidence starts with you.

There are many things you can do to build confidence. Some of them are just small changes to your mindset and others will require you to work harder and longer to create new habits. No matter what, building confidence starts with the decision to *take action*!

Confidence is . . .

▲ Feeling inspired and empowered.

▲ Focusing on controlling the controllable.

▲ Taking responsibility for your actions.

▲ Being comfortable with saying 'no'.

▲ Being open to learning from others.

▲ Stepping out of your comfort zone.

▲ Owning your mistakes.

▲ Accepting compliments.

▲ Freely asking for help.

▲ Being willing to take calculated risks.

The power of affirmations

We've already seen how a single word or sentence has the power to change your life. It can set off a negative mindset or boost your confidence. Self-awareness is at the base of building confidence. It's important to practise using words that help you build your long-term confidence and elevate your life.

Your words become your actions.

Using affirmations is a powerful practice to build high-performance confidence and using these positive phrases or statements helps to challenge negative thoughts that are holding you back. When you repeat them often, believe in them and get emotionally connected to them, you can start to make positive changes and build confidence in who you are and how you show up in the world.

Empower yourself with these affirmations:

▲ 'I am kind and supportive.'
▲ 'I am resilient.'
▲ 'I am open to abundance.'
▲ 'I am deserving of love and respect.'
▲ 'I am a trustworthy friend.'
▲ 'I have the skills to accomplish anything.'
▲ 'I am confident in pursuing that promotion.'
▲ 'I am worthy of success.'

Positive language will have a positive impact on your day and on those around you. You can repeat affirmations multiple times a day, recite them in front of the mirror or write them in your journal to maximise their impact and power.

Take action

Choose your top three affirmations to focus on to help sharpen your performance:

I am healthy	I am truthful	I am grateful
I am brave	I am open	I am kind
I am loved	I am heard	I am funny
I am creative	I am resilient	I am enough
I am clever	I am imperfect	I am graceful
I am strong	I am courageous	I am fearless
I am protected	I am focused on my goals	I am honest
I am abundant	I am self-reliant	I love myself
I am important	I am valuable	I am learning
I am worthy	I am loyal	I am passionate
I am confident		

1. _____

2. _____

3. _____

Affirmations are powerful words, thoughts and habits to practise daily for the rest of your life.

Walk with calm confidence

How you walk into a room says a lot about you. Being confident and calm is the key to elevating your life on your own terms, with clarity, meaning and inner harmony. It is a vital ingredient for personal success and happiness. When we walk with calm and confidence we feel good about ourselves, we are self-assured, have a sense of control and everything seems possible.

Confidence is a skill not a trait and, like all skills, it can be learnt. Upgrading your confidence is not something that you can do overnight; it is a process and takes practice. Remember, confidence is like a muscle and the more you use it the stronger it becomes.

Colleen: Embarking on a remarkable journey from a timid teenager to a self-assured CEO has been a truly transformative and empowering experience for me.

I can vividly recall those early days when I would stand outside the Sportsgirl store in my hometown of Geelong, unable to find the courage to step inside as a shopper. Little did I know then that my path would eventually lead me to become the CEO of this very brand, steering it towards remarkable growth and resounding success. However, this transformation did not occur overnight; it was a journey of perseverance and personal growth.

As a young girl of around thirteen or fourteen, I would gaze longingly through the windows of the Sportsgirl store, plagued by a sense of self-doubt. I convinced myself that I didn't belong. I felt inadequate, believing I wasn't pretty enough, wasn't tall enough and didn't possess the perfect blonde hair. I didn't fit the mould of a size eight, and my introverted nature further intensified my insecurities. In stark contrast, the confident and glamorous sales assistants seemed worlds away from who I was.

Yet, my path towards confidence unfolded gradually, shaped by a lifetime of experiences that propelled me towards a place where I could confidently walk into a boardroom, leaving behind any self-doubt.

Along my journey, I was fortunate to encounter incredible role models who not only supported and guided me, but also pushed me beyond the boundaries of my comfort zone. Their unwavering belief in my abilities played a pivotal role in my confidence-building process, empowering me to silence my inner critic and shatter glass ceilings.

Today, I am thrilled to stand as a role model for you, supporting you in developing your own confidence, recognising your worth, unlocking your potential and elevating your life to extraordinary heights.

Truly, it is amazing what we can achieve when we embrace self-belief.

Confidence summary

1. Confidence is built on the foundation of self-belief and self-worth.
2. A positive mindset fuels confidence and self-motivation.
3. Set boundaries and create habits that align with your values for greater confidence.
4. Train your confidence through regular affirmations.
5. Building confidence starts with the decision to take action.

Create Your Personal High-Performance Plan: CONFIDENCE

What's one thing you want to do but don't have the confidence to?

_____

_____

_____

To elevate your confidence:

What do you need to STOP doing?

1. _____

_____

2. _____

_____

3. _____

_____

What do you need to START doing?

1. _____

_____

2. _____

_____

3. _____

_____

What do you need to KEEP doing?

1. _____

_____

2. _____

_____

3. _____

_____

Pillar 2

LEADERSHIP

Self-Leadership

Self-leadership is the transformative art of guiding and directing yourself towards personal and professional success. It empowers you to take charge of your actions, decisions and mindset, enabling you to become the master of your own destiny.

While self-awareness lays the foundations for personal growth, self-leadership takes it one step further by actively shaping and steering the course of your life.

Through self-leadership, you become the architect of your own path and can embrace the power of influence to lead with purpose, taking ownership of and accountability for the choices you make. It involves developing the necessary skills and adopting empowering habits to effectively lead yourself, even in the face of challenges and uncertainty. Through self-leadership, you unlock the potential to navigate life's twists and turns with resilience and purpose.

Chapter 7

Influence, Inspire, Impact

A leader is one who knows the way, goes the way and shows the way

JOHN MAXWELL

Leadership is something we are both exceptionally passionate about and, when we talk about leadership, we are talking about leading not only in business but also in your own life.

We live in a world where we are conditioned to celebrate and admire people with titles, levels of authority and positions of power. What we have learnt throughout our collective forty-plus-year careers is that a title or rank, the size of your pay packet or the level of authority or position of power doesn't automatically qualify a person for leadership.

In fact, you don't need a title to be a leader. You can be a leader in your family, classroom, community, place of worship, friendship group, neighbourhood or workplace. We all have the ability to elevate in all areas of our lives including the way in which we lead:

- ▲ Supporting someone through challenging times is being a leader.
- ▲ Inspiring and empowering others to elevate is being a leader.
- ▲ Standing up for your ideas and beliefs is being a leader.
- ▲ Encouraging collaboration and teamwork is being a leader.
- ▲ Pushing people outside of their comfort zone is being a leader.

What Is Leadership?

Great leadership is not easy. If it was easy, everyone would be doing it, and they are not. Leading in our own lives is also not easy. It's something you must have an endless pursuit towards achieving – a desire so strong, so passionate and so determined that you take action and commit to living your life purpose and vision.

Great leadership can look different to everyone, and it depends on who you ask as to what kind of answer you get. For us, great leadership encompasses the following:

▲   Being in service to others and prioritising their needs.
▲   Having a passion for a cause that goes beyond personal interests.
▲   Being a leader whom people willingly choose to follow.
▲   Exercising influence through inspiration, not authority.
▲   Demonstrating compassion and courage in leadership actions.
▲   Living in alignment with your values and leading by example.
▲   Inspiring and empowering others to achieve greatness.
▲   Transforming vision into reality.

The best leadership we have ever witnessed is where a person has a passion for a cause that is larger than themselves; where they are selfless, in service to others, are coura- geous, share their vision, show integrity, lead with honesty, live with humility and credit others for the results. They deliver greatness through the way in which they lead others. Great leadership is the ability to motivate people to go places they would never otherwise go. It is about forming genuine connections with the people we get to inspire every day, empowering and guiding them to accomplish their goals and dreams in business and in life.

> Great leadership is the most important competitive advantage an organisation can have.

Only when you are being bold, staying true to your values and feeling empowered yourself can you start to lead others through every decision, every interaction, every reaction and every action that allows you to achieve elevation! Your leadership is an expression of you and the world you want to create and the leadership legacy you want to be remembered for.

There are three 'rules' of leadership that we have built into our values, habits, behaviours, practices and everyday lives:

Rule 1: Lead self

Seventy per cent of leadership is how you lead yourself: how well you know yourself, your values and your purpose; how well you build structure and discipline into your life; how you set goals within your own life; and how you maintain positivity in the face of negativity. It is only when we are leading in our own life that we are truly ready to lead others, become a leader who inspires, influences and makes a positive impact, and a leader who people choose to follow.

Take action

▲ What are you doing to become the leader in your life?
▲ Are you clear on your values and purpose?

Rule 2: Lead others

So many leaders are confused by what it means to manage and lead people as they are often considered to have overlapping functions. The main difference between leaders and managers is that leaders build a vision and have people who follow them, while managers are more operational and have people who work for them.

The difference between leaders and managers

LEADERS . . .	MANAGERS . . .
Empower	Command
Create other leaders	Create followers
Focus on goals	Focus on tasks
Encourage creativity	Encourage conformity
Take risks	Play by the rules
Provide vision	Provide instructions
Think ideas	Think execution
Encourage transformation	Encourage transaction
Create new roads	Follow existing roads

Leading others is having the knowledge, skills, competence and understanding of how to engage, motivate and inspire people. Leading others is about providing resources, training and guidance to escalate others' success. It is also about holding people accountable, creating a vision, having a clear strategy, setting boundaries and pushing leadership down to them so that they can elevate and unlock their true potential.

Take action

▲ Are you a leader or a manager?

▲ Which one do you want to be?

▲ What do you need to change in your life to become that person?

▲ What's one word you would want people to use to describe you?

Rule 3: Lead always

Leadership is not a 'sometimes-on' proposition, for when you're being watched, when you're in the spotlight or when the cameras are on. It's easy to lead when sales are up, your team is winning or the scoreboard is in your favour. Leading always is leading in good times and bad. Leading always is leading when the chips are down: when uncertainly creeps in, when we hit a pandemic, when we have a sales shortfall or when life just isn't going to plan. We always say, 'You don't judge a leader in calm waters.'

Take action

▲ Does your leadership style change depending on who is watching?

▲ How do you react when things are going your way?

▲ What's one thing you can implement to become an always-on leader?

What kind of leader do you want to be? How will you get people to go places they never thought they could go?

Only when you decide what kind of leader you want to be in business and in life, and how you want to show up, can you become that leader.

The Three Pillars for High-Performance Leadership

As we have already mentioned, leadership is not easy. It's something you must be dedicated to, passionate about and work on each day if you want to be best in class, elevate to new heights and be a leader who influences, inspires and makes a positive impact.

Just as being a parent, leading a healthy life or being an athlete are lifestyle choices, so too is being a leader. There are similarities between parenting and leadership, and we have applied many of these parental learnings to our roles as leaders, as well as our everyday lives. As new parents you dive in, often not knowing what the heck you are doing, working it out as you go along. Early leadership can be just like this! When you first become a parent, you don't get a handbook titled *How to be a Great Parent* and away you go. The same goes with becoming a great leader – there is no magic handbook.

No matter how prepared you think you are in the lead-up to becoming a parent, it's only when you're in the role that you learn to really become one. We do use the word *learn* because that's what we did: we learnt every day; we learnt what to do and what not to do; we made mistakes; we cried; we laughed; we lost our confidence and we built our confidence back up again. Our children are now in their late teens and mid-twenties and we are still learning how to be parents every day. You evolve as a parent, just as you evolve as a leader.

Each year of parenthood throws you different challenges and, as your children grow, so do you as a parent. The challenges you have as a parent when your children are toddlers are different from those you have when they are teenagers and different again when they become young adults, but for us the approach has always been the same: teach, guide, coach, nurture, encourage, inspire, empower, build their confidence, let them fall and pick them back up. These are the same guiding principles that we have used throughout our careers and as leaders. Our role as parents and leaders is to create environments where our children feel safe and cared for, so they can thrive and shine. Leadership is a lifestyle choice and one that you choose to be a student of every day.

Like any lifestyle choice, leadership takes practice, discipline and consistency to see great results. The more practice you put in, the more you enhance the results. As leaders, you can't pick and choose which days you feel like giving your best. It's about understanding what kind of leader you want to be, showing up with intention, holding yourself to an elite standard and being consistent.

Leadership is not just about being in charge. It's about having the power to influence, inspire and make a lasting impact:

INFLUENCE

Great leadership is influence, not authority

Empower your people
Build long-lasting trust
Connect with emotions
Be assertive, not aggressive
Lead by example
Communicate the vision
Give people a voice
Teach your knowledge

INSPIRE

Inspiring others unlocks their untapped potential

Be the role model
Lead with purpose
Lift up others
Create bold goals
Walk with calm confidence
Keep your word
Stay true to yourself
Lead with kindness

IMPACT

You were born to have an impact

Give back
Mentor others
Go the extra mile
Be innovative

Lead with pure optimism
Live a courageous life
Be fully present
Celebrate others' wins

Influence

Influence is an important leadership quality because it means people will listen to and follow you. Influence typically means to affect or change someone. Great leaders do this in a positive way, helping people become better versions of themselves today than they were yesterday. Influential leaders also tend to be more trusted and effective.

Empower your people

There is no greater way to influence people than by empowering and supporting them with the words 'I believe in you.' When you believe in someone, it helps them to find an inner strength they didn't know they had. It fosters engagement, builds confidence and promotes innovation. When you believe in someone, you inspire them to elevate and unlock their potential and even sometimes achieve the impossible.

> Great leadership is about genuine influence, not authority. It is through this influence that leaders can ignite positive change and guide individuals to reach their full potential.

Build long-lasting trust

Influence is most often and easily built through trust. Trust is the foundation that must first be built if you want to create healthy and influential working environments and relationships. The easiest way to build trust is through open and honest communication. Building trust is about creating positive relationships, demonstrating expertise and judgement, and delivering consistency.

Connect with emotions

Talking to each other, sharing your joys and sorrows, trusting each other, showing affection and being weak and vulnerable with each other, are a few ways we can connect with emotions. This strong connectivity of emotions within the workplace leads to an increase in communication and deeper relationships. Leaders of influence empower individuals to embrace their authentic selves in the workplace by promoting open communication, valuing everyone's perspectives and creating an inclusive environment where individuals feel heard and respected.

Be assertive, not aggressive

Assertive leaders present their thoughts and ideas with confidence, conviction and self-belief in a way that influences others. Being assertive means expressing yourself in an open, honest way; it's being authentic in the way you communicate your values, opinions and feelings. Aggressive behaviour is emotionally charged, lacks consideration and empathy for others and often ends in insult. This is not the way to influence others.

Lead by example

Leading by example is about leaders setting the tone. They act in a way that shows others how to act. They must be good role models and walk the walk if they want people to follow. If leaders want to inspire and empower their people a 'do as I say, not as I do' leadership style is not going to cut it. This will make people resentful, disengage and have little or no respect for their leader. We have always tried to lead by example and would never ask anything of our teams that we would not be prepared to do ourselves. Leaders who lead by example make it easier for others to follow them.

Communicate the vision

As a leader, it is crucial to the success of your organisation to share your vision (see page 71). It provides a sense of purpose and direction and helps with decision-making. How can people know what to do when they don't know where they are going? If leaders want people on their bus, then they need to know the journey ahead.

Give people a voice

Great ideas don't just come from the top. Create a safe environment where every level of the organisation is encouraged to speak up and have a voice. When people know their voice is heard they are more open to sharing ideas, knowledge and skills. Leaders create an inclusive environment where everyone's perspectives and contributions are valued and heard, which also builds open and trusting relationships, and can contribute to an organisation's success.

Teach your knowledge

When we stop learning, we stop growing. You have stories, experiences, learnings, failures and successes that are unique to you, so share them. When you do, the people around you will grow and flourish through your knowledge. Not only will this increase the skills in your organisation, but it will help your people feel more connected.

Inspire

To inspire others is to excite, encourage, generate confidence, be selfless and creative, and dare to be different. People who inspire us are people we look up to or admire, or those we would like to emulate. Richard Branson identifies the ability to inspire as the single most important skill.

Be the role model

A positive role model is someone who is worthy of imitation and motivates you by modelling a guide to achieving success. Having a positive role model in leadership and life inspires us to do our best. Role models do this through a clear set of values, an acceptance of others and their ability to overcome obstacles.

Lead with purpose

Leaders who inspire us live each day with intention and purpose, and encourage others to do the same. Having a sense of purpose is knowing that your life is valuable, meaningful and important. Living with purpose makes a positive impact and inspires those around you. Purpose not only gives our lives meaning, but it also moves us from 'what we do' to 'why we do it' and our purpose is the reason we show up each day. (See page 177 for more on identifying your purpose.)

Lift up others

Great leaders inspire and create future leaders. They do this by building and lifting up others and helping them elevate and reach their full potential. They encourage them to share their ideas, think big, acknowledge their efforts and provide them with opportunities to grow. Building up others not only inspires individual elevation but also elevates teams. High-performing individuals create high-performing teams.

Create bold goals

Inspiring others to set bold goals is a powerful way to ignite their passion and drive. By sharing your ambitious aspirations, you lead by example and encourage others to dream big. This creates a ripple effect of motivation, fostering a culture of innovation and resilience where individuals fearlessly pursue their aspirations, ultimately changing lives and the world.

Walk with calm confidence

Inspiring others to embrace challenges and opportunities with calm confidence is an impactful form of leadership. It is a quiet yet powerful belief in oneself and a commitment to never giving up. By setting such an example, we assist others in cultivating trust in their own abilities and confidence in their capacity to succeed.

Keep your word

Keeping your word is to do what you promise to do. It's that simple. Keeping your word as a leader lays the foundations for trust, credibility and respect. For example, if you agree to provide regular feedback and support, keeping your word involves delivering on that promise. It means scheduling feedback sessions, offering guidance and providing resources for growth and development. Failing to keep your word communicates a lack of integrity and erodes confidence.

Stay true to yourself

When you stay true to who you are, you are being honest with what you feel, deeply value and desire. It also means *behaving according to your beliefs*. Staying true to who you are means you do not have to sacrifice and betray your own identity. When we live and lead in this way, we feel energised and fulfilled. No matter how hard life or leadership gets, stay true to yourself.

Lead with kindness

As we'll explore in Chapter 10, kindness is generosity of spirit that enables leaders to be empathetic, good listeners, inspire and build confidence in others. Leading with kindness is understanding what inspires people, what they are good at, where they want to grow and showing you're there for them, care for them, understand them and value them through the way you lead with kindness.

Impact

Impact means being someone people remember – through our actions, words, confidence, kindness and ability to influence and inspire.

You were born to have an impact.

It is about using the resources available to us – regardless of our position or wealth – to have a lasting and positive impact on ourselves and our family, friends, colleagues, organisations and society. Leadership is not about authority; it is about the courage to be different and the willingness to lift up others and make a positive impact on those around us. Leadership affects our everyday interactions and experiences. As leaders in our own lives, everything we say and do has an impact on us and those around us.

Give back

When we give back, we create a positive ripple effect. You may be in a position to help others who are less fortunate than you – perhaps through generous gifting or by giving leadership advice, your time or love. Even small gestures, like offering your time and support, can have a positive impact on the lives of others and inspire kindness and generosity in others.

Mentor others

Mentoring someone allows you to guide, support, challenge, inspire and develop another person's skills. We can all be a mentor, because we are all good at something. As a mentor, you can help others in areas you are knowledgeable and passionate about. By being a mentor to someone you can have an everlasting impact on their future and elevate their leadership and life journey.

Go the extra mile

Great leaders go the extra mile by doing more than is required. They exceed expectations and go beyond the call of duty to support those around them. They see difficult situations as a chance to learn and discover new ways of doing things, and inspire those around them to do the same.

Going above and beyond is commonly associated with a strong work ethic, which entails valuing and exemplifying dedication and high-quality work, while maintaining a healthy work–life balance.

Be innovative

Inspiring leaders invite innovation and creativity to lead people and manage projects. They inspire productivity in new ways and through different approaches. Innovative leaders help others create a vision, while being able to envision the future as well as the benefits of innovation. Innovative leaders encourage, inspire and motivate people to innovate and create the change necessary to shape future success.

Lead with pure optimism

Optimism is an incredibly valuable leadership skill as it creates a future vision that can inspire others to do whatever it takes to get there. Optimism fuels the achievement of long-term goals and equal effort in reaching them. Optimism is contagious and, when we lead in this way in our workplace, our home and our community, it has a positive ripple effect on those around us.

Live a courageous life

To be courageous means that you are able to act in spite of feeling fearful and this inspires others to be courageous. Being courageous means having a growth mindset (see page 80), being passionate, resilient, bold, never giving up and believing the impossible is possible. It is this courage that allows us to be vulnerable, build confidence, embrace our failures and learn from our mistakes. Courage means always doing what is right, not what is easy or popular.

Be fully present

The difference between a good leader and a great leader lies in their capacity to genuinely listen and appreciate the opinions, ideas and perspectives of others. This skill can only be honed when one is fully present in the moment. It's crucial to remember that, while you're engaged in speaking, you are unable to actively listen. By embracing the art of active listening, you can elevate your leadership abilities and foster stronger connections with those around you.

Celebrate others' wins

There is courage in celebrating and embracing others' success, and we have made celebrating each other's wins a powerful habit.

Contemporary leadership involves:

▲ Sharing information openly.
▲ Building trust among team members.
▲ Promoting inclusion and a sense of belonging.
▲ Creating safe environments for voicing opinions and challenging norms.
▲ Cultivating a culture of creativity and innovation.
▲ Inspiring and empowering others.
▲ Encouraging collaboration and trust.
▲ Putting people at the heart of everything you do.

Leading in Your Own Life

We believe that each of you can be a leader in your own lives. Whether you are a CEO, a parent, a partner, a business owner, an entrepreneur, a coach, an athlete or a community worker, you can choose and craft the type of leader you want to be for a high-performance life.

Leading in your own life is about self-awareness, self-leadership, self-management and being in the pursuit of becoming the best version of yourself and adopting a mindset of personal life mastery. Those who rise, raise the bar, embrace courage, supercharge their actions and have an unwavering commitment to showing up as their best version every day can have an extraordinary life of fulfilment, happiness, achievement and success.

Leading in your own life comes from the commitment to self-development and being the director of your personal journey. It is your ability to stretch, to shift your motivation to a higher gear, to persist and to always be a student of life. It requires inner focus and tuning in with great awareness into the business of YOU. It means taking full control of the actions, reactions, interactions and decisions you make. It means upgrading your attitude and being the CEO in your own life.

Next-level leadership

There are many things you can do to elevate your life and leadership and take it to the next level, and we'll be exploring these in the chapters that follow. Next-level leadership is a joy ride to jump on, a challenge to set yourself to raise your own bar first. Through developing leadership skills, you will learn to elevate the way you feel, the way you communicate and the way you interact with others. Being a leader is leading self-first and developing personal strategies to enhance your life, no matter what your profession or age, so you can live an ever-evolving, ultra-inspiring life.

Leadership
Empathy
Authentic
Discipline
Empower
Resilience
Strategic
Humility
Inspire
Passion

Colleen: My leadership style evolved very early in my career. I didn't realise it at the time, but I was very purposefully becoming a leader by design. I wasn't consciously thinking about the end game; I just followed my heart and my instincts, and this led me to become the type of leader I always wanted to be.

People and relationships were always important to me, and I could see the impact that putting people *first* could make. I have never been a leader who feared my team being better, smarter or more skilled than me – in fact, I strived for it. I believed having incredible people around me was one of my biggest advantages as a leader. Throughout my thirty-year career I have met leaders at different levels and from different industries with fear in their eyes – scared of being outdone, outshone or outsmarted. I always saw this as a reflection of their own insecurities.

In this profit-driven world we live in today, it's no surprise that sales, margins, shareholder returns and revenue are at the forefront of most leaders' minds. At the end of the day, profit is essential for all businesses, both big and small, to keep the doors open and allow for reinvestment and growth. But I want to challenge the traditional business focus we have become accustomed to. My secret weapon is: *people with purpose and passion = profit.*

I have always aimed to create environments where people get up every day and come to work feeling safe, valued, inspired, empowered and fulfilled, and feel part of something bigger than just themselves. I believe this has been one of the biggest success factors for me as a leader.

Shannah: High-performance leadership is personal for me as I do not have a team of employees. As a coach, I lead through listening and providing a safe space for people to explore how they can elevate their lives and then asking powerful questions that empower them to make change.

I lead with the resources I have and with the attitude I bring to my clients, family, friends and networks. I set a standard of conduct for myself, work constantly on my vision, goals, habits and plans, and know I am a student of life and always learning. I too hope my actions inspire, impact and influence others to elevate in life.

Leadership summary

1. Leadership is a mindset, a heart set, a behaviour, a feeling and a way of being.
2. Leadership is showing empathy, compassion and courage to self and others.
3. Leadership sits under the three pillars of influence, inspire and impact.
4. Leadership is being someone people choose to follow.
5. Leadership is about clarity of communication.

Create Your Personal High-Performance Plan: LEADERSHIP

Write three leadership words on how you want to show up:

_____

_____

_____

To elevate your leadership journey:

What do you need to STOP doing?

1. _____
   _____
2. _____
   _____
3. _____
   _____

What do you need to START doing?

1. _____
   _____
2. _____
   _____
3. _____
   _____

What do you need to KEEP doing?

1. _____
   _____
2. _____
   _____
3. _____
   _____

Chapter 8

Discover Your Personal Brand

Your brand is what people say about you when you are not in the room

JEFF BEZOS

To stand out from the crowd, it's essential to have a strong personal brand. Your personal brand is an expression of your unique identity, skills and experiences.

In your professional life, effective personal branding will differentiate you from the competition, showcase your reputation and allow you to build trust with prospective clients and employers. Personal branding is an extremely important professional tool, yet it's one many of us say we don't have time for. But neglecting it means getting left behind while others are overtaking and making meaningful impact and progress in their lives and careers. Your personal branding is part of a strong business strategy that will allow you to connect with customers authentically and identify yourself as a professional in the industry.

In your personal life, your brand is a lifelong project that constantly evolves and changes. And there are many ways to develop a personal brand, but it begins with knowing who you are and what your values are. Your personal brand is nothing less than your reputation; the mental notes people make when they meet, talk about and think of you. Define it well, earn it diligently, promote it positively and you will have an asset that pays dividends over a lifetime.

Everyone has a personal brand – including you. It pops up on Google when someone searches you, and your presence on social media shows how authentic you are across all platforms and in all areas of your life. It encapsulates your passion, unique selling proposition, brand positioning, story and talents, as well as who you authentically are.

> Your brand is both what you stand for and what you do.

Advantages of a Personal Brand

Helps you to stand out

Having a strong personal brand means identifying what makes you stand out and allowing this to transcend through everything you do. Having a unique personal brand makes you someone people remember while also elevating your reputation and career.

Expresses your passion

Personal branding is a way to express your passions and interests through your work. It's like showcasing your superpowers in how you connect with others and sharing what truly lights you up. Personal branding means making sure your job reflects your unique personality. And when your work lets you be your authentic self while making a positive difference in people's lives and the world around you . . . that is truly magical!

Elevates your authenticity

Cultivating your personal brand empowers you to consistently present yourself in a way that's uniquely genuine to who you are. Authentic leaders are not only a source of inspiration but also radiate compassion and foster trust that extends throughout an entire organisation. Embracing your personal brand in an authentic way becomes a testament to your passion, boosts your energy and reflects who you want to become.

Puts you in the driver's seat

When you have a strong personal brand, you are in the driver's seat of your life and your career. You can let life just happen around you, or you can take control and create, with intention and purpose, the career and life you want for yourself. When you are the driver in your own life, you get to choose how fast or slow you go, what roads you go down and who you invite to be your passengers in life. When you are the driver in your own life you can also ask people to get off the journey if they are not interested in heading in the same direction.

Builds a confident you

When you clearly define your personal brand, it allows you to have great self-awareness and step into your confident self. As your personal brand grows so will your confidence because you have clearly defined what you do, why you do it and why it matters. Confidence pays off on so many levels: new opportunities, recognition, acknowledgement, personal growth and success.

Makes you a brand authority

Personal branding allows you to position yourself and your brand as an authority in your industry, differentiating from your competition and increasing your reputation. A brand authority is viewed as trustworthy, relevant, an expert in their field, respected and has a high level of influence within the industry that results in incredible loyalty and reward.

Controls your narrative

Your personal brand story must cohesively encompass and define your purpose, beliefs and values. You need to control the narrative around your personal branding. If you don't define yourself, then someone else will define you, and it may not be the way you want the world to see you.

Attracts opportunities

Once you are clear on exactly what your brand proposition is and are ready to share it with the world, you will start to grow exponentially through the way you differentiate and express your authentic self. People will feel more connected to you and start to pay attention. If you stay authentic and true to yourself, there will be no limit to your brand's potential.

Builds wealth

People are willing to pay for strong brands. We all want connection and experiences in life and people are prepared to pay for it. Powerful brands can name their price because it's not necessarily about the product — it's about an emotional connection on a much deeper level. Your strong personal brand will allow you to earn more because you are delivering an authentic, unique offering or experience that connects.

Take action

▲ How do you stand out?

▲ How authentic are you being?

▲ Do you feel like you are in the driver's seat?

▲ What are you an expert in?

▲ Are you open to opportunities?

▲ Are you valuing the worth of your skills?

Identifying Your Purpose

Identifying your purpose is crucial for developing your personal brand. It goes beyond just what you do; it's the underlying reason behind your actions and existence. Discovering your purpose means finding the deeper meaning and significance in your life. It reflects your core values, passions and the impact you want to make in the world. Your purpose is what drives you, guides your career and life choices, and helps you create a meaningful and fulfilling life. When you align your personal brand with your purpose, it becomes a powerful tool that communicates who you are and what you stand for. It helps you differentiate yourself, build credibility and attract the right opportunities. Your purpose supports and enhances the development of your personal brand, making it an integral part of your overall success.

While your vision, which we explored in Chapter 3, provides a specific target to strive for, your purpose acts as a guiding principle throughout your journey, influencing your choices and helping you stay true to your authentic self as you pursue your vision.

Understanding the relationship between your purpose and vision is essential in creating a personal brand that is aligned with your values, resonates with others and ultimately leads to a fulfilling and purpose-driven life. By uncovering your purpose, you can create a powerful personal brand that reflects who you are, what you stand for and the positive impact you want to make in the world.

We want you to think for a moment of a brand that you believe has a strong purpose; one that has a strong belief and reason for being that goes beyond what it sells.

Powerful purpose = powerful brand.

A brand that has a strong purpose:

▲ Adds value to both customers and broader society.
▲ Builds emotional relationships with the consumer.
▲ Is differentiated from its competitors through its purpose.
▲ Builds a connection beyond what it sells.

Apple is synonymous with *innovation*, Dove with *confidence* and Patagonia with *saving the planet*. These brands not only have name recognition, but they're also powerful examples of brands that are world class, connect on a deep level, differentiate and have a strong purpose and reason for being beyond what they sell. They connect with their consumers in a meaningful way and are deeply desired.

Eight tips on defining your purpose

1. **Reflect on your values and passions:** Take time for introspection and reflect on your core values and passions. Consider what brings you joy, fulfilment and a sense of meaning. Think about the activities or causes that resonate deeply with you and where you feel most aligned with your authentic self.

2. **Recognise your personal strengths:** Revisit Chapter 1 where you identified your unique strengths, talents and skills. Consider the areas in which you excel and the qualities that come naturally to you. Aligning your purpose with your strengths allows you to leverage your abilities and make a meaningful impact.

3. **Explore your life experiences:** Reflect on significant experiences in your life that have shaped you or made a profound impact. Identify patterns or themes that emerge from those experiences. They may provide valuable insight into your purpose and the areas where you can contribute most effectively.

4. **Clarify your impact and contribution:** Consider the kind of impact you want to make in the world (see page 162 for more on this) and how you wish to contribute to the lives of others. Reflect on the causes, issues or communities that you are passionate about and where you believe you can create positive change.

5. **Seek inspiration:** Seek inspiration from others who have found their purpose or are making a difference in areas that align with your interests. Read biographies, watch TED Talks, listen to podcasts or engage in conversations with individuals who inspire you. Their stories and experiences can provide guidance and inspiration for your own journey.

6. **Experiment and explore:** Take action and explore different areas of interest. Engage in volunteer work, join organisations or communities related to your passions, or pursue new hobbies and projects. By actively participating and experimenting, you can gain valuable insight into what resonates with you and what doesn't.

7. **Embrace a growth mindset:** Embrace a growth mindset (see page 80) and view the process of discovering your purpose as a continuous journey. Be open to learning, adapting and evolving. Allow yourself to explore different paths and be willing to make adjustments along the way as you gain new insights and experiences.

8. **Listen to your inner voice:** Take time to quieten your mind and trust your instincts. Your intuition knows what truly matters to you. Connect with your inner self through solitude and introspection. This will help you gain clarity on your purpose. Embrace the journey of self-discovery and trust the process.

Defining your purpose is a personal and ongoing process. It may take time and self-reflection to gain clarity. Be patient with yourself and trust that, as you engage in actions aligned with your purpose, you will gain a deeper understanding and refine your sense of purpose over time.

We have provided an example of a purpose statement below to inspire you:

To be an authentic human who creates a positive impact in people's lives. I aim to inspire and empower others, helping them build confidence, take charge of their own lives, practise kindness and strive to become their best selves.

Brand purpose

Just as your purpose is important to help define your personal brand, brand purpose is also imperative for organisations if they want to build trust, loyalty and create meaningful and lasting relationships with consumers. Consumers are increasingly becoming more conscious and considering brand purpose when deciding whether to purchase a service or product. Today's consumer cares less about the product or service they are paying for, and more about what kind of impact a brand is making in the world. This means that your brand purpose can have a major impact on how your organisation is viewed, and a powerful brand purpose will differentiate, build reputation and lead market share with growth and success.

In essence, brand purpose is a brand's reason for existing, beyond financial incentives. Brands that have a strong purpose connect with their consumers on a much deeper emotional level.

Building Attributes for Your Personal Brand

Determining your brand attributes is crucial to help establish an authentic personal brand aligned with your purpose. It requires self-awareness and reflection to understand your unique qualities and values. Your brand attributes should closely align with your purpose, reflecting the deeper meaning behind your actions. By consistently embodying these attributes, you differentiate yourself from others and build trust. Clarity in your messaging is enhanced when you articulate what you stand for and why you're here.

Ultimately, aligning your brand attributes with your purpose enables you to make a meaningful impact, attracting like-minded individuals and opportunities. By shaping your personal brand authentically, you build powerful connections.

Asking questions is a powerful tool in the process of finding and building attributes for developing your personal brand. It is through questioning that you gain deeper insight into yourself, your unique strengths and what sets you apart. Questions prompt you to reflect and uncover valuable aspects of your character and preferences. Questions serve as a catalyst for self-discovery, helping you define and refine the attributes that shape your personal brand. They guide you towards clarity, authenticity and the ability to effectively communicate who you are and what you stand for.

Self-reflection = self-awareness.

Consider the questions below:

What makes you indispensable?	
In what ways do you provide value?	
How are you differentiating?	
Do you lead or follow a crowd?	
Do you like to try new things?	
When was the last time you read a book?	
How do you communicate your values?	
Are you networking?	
What is your style of clothing?	
What are the big ideas in your head?	
Do you enjoy your job or are you going through the motions?	
What new things are you learning?	
Do you reflect?	
When was the last time you failed?	
When was the last time you tried something new?	
When you don't know the answer to something do you google it?	
What successful people do you admire and model?	
What do you bring to the world that is truly yours?	

Take the time to reflect on the answers to the questions. Identify recurring themes, patterns and strengths that emerge from your responses. This self-awareness will help you understand your unique qualities and attributes, which will inform your personal brand. Below is a step-by-step guide to help you create your brand statement:

Six Steps to Defining Your Personal Brand

Step 1: Define your unique value proposition

Based on the insights gained above, determine how you provide value to others. Consider the skills, experiences and perspectives that set you apart. Craft a clear and concise statement that communicates your unique value proposition to your target audience.

Step 2: Shape your story

Use the information gathered to develop your personal narrative. Share your experiences, challenges and triumphs that have shaped you into who you are today. Craft a compelling story that authentically represents your journey and showcases your values and strengths.

Step 3: Identify your differentiators

Look for aspects that differentiate you from others in your field or industry. Highlight your unique strengths, perspectives or approaches that make you stand out. Emphasise these differentiators in your personal brand to attract attention and create a memorable impression.

Step 4: Find your style

Embrace the process of discovering and refining a style that truly represents your authentic self, aligns with your personal brand and complements your brand message, allowing you to confidently present yourself to the world as the unique individual you are.

Step 5: Consistency and alignment

Ensure that your personal brand aligns with your values, passions and long-term goals. Consistency is key in building a strong and authentic personal brand. Align your actions, words and online presence with the attributes and values you want to be known for.

Step 6: Communicate your brand

Utilise various channels, such as social media platforms, professional networking events or personal websites, to communicate your personal brand. Develop a strong online presence and engage with your target audience, sharing your story, expertise and insights. Consistently reinforce your brand message and values through your communication channels.

Remember, developing a personal brand is an ongoing process. Continuously reassess and refine your brand as you grow personally and professionally. Stay true to your authentic self and consistently communicate your unique attributes to build a strong and impactful personal brand.

There is only one you and your brand is the unique combination of skills and experiences that make you who you are. This is how you present yourself to the world – it is in your control.

Colleen: As a CEO for thirteen years, brand equity, DNA and purpose were always at the heart of my decision-making. When everyone in an organisation is connected to your brand purpose and identity it allows people to be empowered to make decisions with confidence and for the organisation to be successful.

As for my own personal brand and purpose, my purpose has evolved over the years, just as I have. That said, I always knew I wanted to help people. I wanted to inspire and empower others through my leadership and my own story and experiences. My personal brand has also evolved and become a big part of my values, personality, appearance, the way I communicate and how I show up in the world.

My brand statement now looks like this:

I'm a visionary leader, inspiring and empowering others to embrace their uniqueness and reach their potential. From leaving school at sixteen to becoming CEO of an iconic Australian brand, my journey embodies determination and resilience. With my distinctive style of black attire and stylish glasses, I offer a unique and refreshing approach to leadership. As a leader people choose to follow, I foster a culture of collaboration, growth and kind leadership. Through mentoring, books and keynote speaking, I share my story and expertise, inspiring others to overcome challenges and achieve greatness. Join me in revolutionising fashion with authenticity and inclusivity.

Brand summary

1. Personal branding is about expressing your authentic self and your values.
2. Defining your personal brand elevates success in your career and life.
3. Your personal brand starts with self-awareness.
4. Brand purpose is a brand's reason for existing, beyond financial incentives.
5. Elevate using the six steps to define your personal brand.

Create Your Personal High-Performance Plan: BRAND

Write out your brand statement:

_____

_____

_____

To elevate your personal brand:

What do you need to STOP doing?

1. _____

_____

2. _____

_____

3. _____

_____

What do you need to START doing?

1. _____

_____

2. _____

_____

3. _____

_____

What do you need to KEEP doing?

1. _____

_____

2. _____

_____

3. _____

_____

Chapter 9

Establish an
Empowered Culture

Culture is what motivates
and retains talented
employees

BETTY THOMPSON

Establishing a strong, inspiring and empowering culture isn't something you can do easily. There is no magic pill for a great culture. Culture is not something you can buy off the shelf, nor will a few affirmations or posters around the office do the trick. Creating a strong culture is something you must work at every single day.

All of this might make it sound like establishing an empowered culture is a lot of work – and we're going to be honest, it is. But it's also a very worthwhile investment because the dividends and pay-off of a positive, productive, inspiring and empowering workplace culture are immeasurable.

What Is 'Culture'?

Culture can be such a difficult concept to define. It relates to people, purpose and the organisation itself, and how they are all intertwined.

Some might say that culture has to do with people from different nationalities, and this is right – to a certain degree. Culture includes race, nationality, cultural backgrounds and ethnicity, but it goes far beyond those identity markers as well.

When we talk about culture, we refer to it as 'way of life'. It encompasses beliefs, values, practices, attitudes and behaviours that people share – not only in the workplace, but in many areas of our lives, including family life, community, place of worship, hobbies and even sporting clubs. Culture must be taught, learnt and nurtured.

From an organisational perspective, culture is the environment that you create for your employees. Creating a great culture is not about free lunches, free parking or a free pass to the gym, although all of these things are nice to have. These are more like perks. If you are responsible for people, you are also responsible for establishing a culture that allows people to thrive and shine, and work at their natural best. It also plays a powerful role in their work satisfaction, retention, relationships, performance and progression, not to mention the positive impact it can have on revenue and profit.

Ten signs of a great workplace culture

1. Transparent communication.
2. A diverse and inclusive workforce.
3. Wins are celebrated.
4. A clear vision and values.
5. Positive working relationships.
6. High level of innovation.
7. Accessible leadership teams.
8. Employee empowerment.
9. Collaboration encouraged.
10. High levels of trust.

Creating a culture of openness, empowerment, collaboration, trust and cooperation is the foundation of a thriving organisation.

Why is culture important?

Workplace culture impacts everything from performance to how an organisation is perceived, both internally and externally. A great culture reflects the organisation's vision, objectives, expectations and values that guide its behaviours and motivate everyone to do their best work.

Building a great culture in your organisation will also help you to entice and retain top talent, and improve employee engagement, productivity and performance – all things that drive an organisation to success and greatness.

Employees want to know why the organisation exists and what makes it different from its competitors. Only then can potential employees decide if your organisation is aligned to their values and something they would like to be a part of.

In our experience, creating a positive culture makes for happier people who are more committed, have greater job satisfaction, perform better, collaborate and are more likely to stay and grow with the organisation.

A great culture . . .

upholds strong values

communicates a clear vision

emphasises fairness and respect

cultivates trust and cooperation

values everyone's opinions

embraces individual strengths

celebrates diversity

attracts top talent

sparks positive action

rewards teamwork

Take action

Before you can elevate your culture, it is important to be able to articulate what kind of culture resides inside your organisation:

▲ What are the core values and beliefs that define your culture?

▲ How do people in your organisation behave and interact?

▲ What is the overall energy and enthusiasm like within the organisation?

▲ How are decisions made and conflicts resolved?

▲ How inclusive, diverse and open is your organisation?

▲ Are you adaptable and open to change?

These simplified prompts can help you gain insights into the current culture of your organisation and identify areas for potential improvement or transformation.

Ten Ways to Create a Great Workplace Culture

A positive culture is something so simple and we all recognise it as important, yet it's difficult for many organisations and leaders to implement. Many leaders talk about their competitive advantage as being their strategy, process, product, innovation and HR policies. While this might be true to some extent, we believe an organisation's biggest competitive advantage is its people and the culture and environment they work in.

So, why do so many organisations struggle to create cultures that engage their people? This is a problem we have constantly wrestled to understand, and our mission is to buck that trend.

There is no easy road to creating a great culture: if there was, everyone would have it right, and most don't. Each culture is unique to an organisation, just like each of us is unique as individuals. It takes a clear focus, commitment and consistency to establish a positive culture, but with the right strategies in place you can create a culture of high performance that sets you apart from your competitors.

Here is our recipe for building a successful culture that inspires and empowers!

1. Set clear expectations

Employees need to have a clear understanding of what the company expects from them. This requires effective communication and clarity so people can fully align themselves with the expectations, guidelines, boundaries and rules. By ensuring clear expectations, people are empowered to meet and exceed those standards, contributing to a positive and productive work environment.

2. Recognise achievements

Recognition refers to the ways in which an organisation shows its appreciation for employees' contributions and recognises people's achievements. This can be one of the greatest motivators to drive engagement.

Recognising and rewarding employees for achieving outstanding results encourages them to maintain high performance and makes them feel valued within the organisation. Having their hard work and achievement recognised fuels people to strive for improvement and also motivates others to perform at their best, creating a culture of friendly competition that results in improved performance.

3. Ensure their work matters

Employees want their work to be meaningful and to make a difference in their company and communities. When they don't feel this, they can become disenchanted and dissatisfied.

Employees want to feel bigger than just the seat they sit in, and want to know that their contributions are having a positive impact. When people feel encouraged, supported and listened to, they will do amazing things!

4. Encourage relationship-building

Successful organisations know the value of fostering positive relationships between people and teams. When people feel like 'one team' they can accomplish great things together. People can share their ideas, expertise and learn from each other: 'One team, one dream.'

When you encourage relationship-building, this also leads to increased communication across different parts of your organisation. The key to encouraging relationship-building is providing opportunities for people to connect in less formal settings.

5. Encourage 'life in balance'

When employees take care of their well-being, they perform better at work. We believe that work and life should harmoniously coexist and complement each other. Encouraging work–life balance not only fosters a healthier, happier and more productive workforce, but also reduces stress and helps prevent burnout. It's a win-win situation for everyone involved.

6. Be flexible

Particularly over the past few years, many companies have come to understand the importance of flexible working arrangements.

We all know that life is full of unexpected things. Employees need to know that they can attend to emergencies or responsibilities outside of work without concerns or repercussions. For some it might be struggling to balance work with their family life; for others it could be their health or personal life.

Being flexible can improve morale, drive engagement and reduce turnover. When you look after the people, the people look after you and your organisation.

7. Live your values

Values are not just a list of words on the wall in the staff kitchen or the 'About' page on your website. Values are your organisation's North Star, code of conduct and inner compass. Values set the tone for how the organisation behaves. Your values are aligned to the organisation's vision and goals and are the lighthouse for all the decision-making. Your organisational values (see page 54) need to be shared at every level of the organisation if you are to truly live and breathe them.

8. Welcome feedback

Many leaders find it hard to give feedback, not to mention receive it. Some organisations believe that conducting half-yearly or yearly performance reviews is enough. Well, we are here to tell you it's not! Employees want clear and concise feedback on a regular basis allowing them to also share their thoughts, achievements and concerns. People want to know what is expected of them, how their performance is tracking against where they were previously and what their future holds.

9. Set a career roadmap

A career roadmap is an essential part of career progression, as well as personal growth and development. A roadmap with clear goals and desired outcomes ensures employees stay on track. A roadmap is important in retaining talented employees and keeping them engaged, and, more importantly, creating future leaders. Setting your employees up for success means providing the right tools, resources, support, training and goals for them to achieve their upward growth and career ambitions.

10. Promote diversity and inclusivity

Diversity and inclusivity should be paramount priorities for every organisation. By fostering a diverse workplace, you recognise and leverage the individual strengths of employees from various racial, ethnic, socioeconomic and cultural backgrounds, as well as lifestyles, experiences and interests. This inclusive environment cultivates a work culture where everyone feels equally heard and engaged.

An effective inclusivity strategy appreciates and values the unique qualities of each employee. It promotes transparency, accountability and a wide range of perspectives, ensuring equal access to opportunities for all. By embracing diversity and fostering inclusivity, organisations not only enhance the employee experience but also promote improved productivity, more effective decision-making processes and a positive reputation.

Establish open communication, encourage active listening and create participation opportunities. Leaders should seek input, lead by example and ensure psychological safety. With everyone's voice heard and respected, organisations foster a culture of employee satisfaction and success.

Keep it light and fun

Establishing a great culture requires keeping it light and fun. This boosts employee morale, engagement and productivity. To achieve this, organisations can encourage open communication, promote team bonding, recognise achievements, incorporate fun elements and maintain life in balance (see page 274). Leaders play a crucial role in setting the tone, leading with a positive attitude and fostering a culture of respect. A light and fun workplace culture attracts and retains talented individuals, contributing to overall success and satisfaction.

A strong culture is the cornerstone for creating a positive and thriving work environment where individuals can reach their full potential and organisations can achieve their goals.

Shannah: I am very privileged to have the opportunity to work with great leaders and CEOs and observe the culture of their businesses. Athletes who are a part of sporting teams also share the culture aspect with me, both good and bad, and a culture can heavily influence their height of success.

A culture that fosters growth, inclusivity, diversity, open communication, feedback, support and pathways to upgrade their skills through training and coaching, and most importantly celebrates achievements, always retains the best employees and gets the reputation of a workplace of choice. As Colleen's coach I witnessed and was a part of this process. The culture was exceptional, the loyalty to leader and brand fierce, and people came before profit always.

Culture summary

1. Culture is a 'way of life'. It encompasses beliefs, values, practices, attitudes and behaviours that people share.
2. The environment you create for your employees has an impact on how they describe the organisation.
3. Culture plays a powerful role in employees' work satisfaction, retention, relationships, performance and progression.
4. To create a healthy culture for your organisation you need to first envisage what this will look like.
5. Culture is what people do when no one is watching.

Create Your Personal High-Performance Plan: CULTURE

Define what an inspiring and empowering culture looks like for your organisation:

_____

_____

_____

To elevate your culture:

What do you need to STOP doing?

1. _____

   _____

2. _____

   _____

3. _____

   _____

What do you need to START doing?

1. _____

   _____

2. _____

   _____

3. _____

   _____

What do you need to KEEP doing?

1. _____

   _____

2. _____

   _____

3. _____

   _____

Chapter 10

Cultivate Kindness

It takes courage to be kind

MAYA ANGELOU

W hat's the first word that comes to mind when you think of great leadership? Do you visualise power? Strength? Direction? Drive? Focus? Perseverance?

Well, we are here to challenge that. We strongly believe that leading with kindness is what will separate good leaders from the great leaders of the future. Kindness is often seen as a sign of weakness, but we believe the opposite. We believe that kindness requires courage and strength, and that leading with kindness is more important than ever in leadership and life.

You may have heard of – or worse, experienced first-hand – situations of bullying, intimidation or dealing with difficult people in the workplace. This kind of behaviour can be very destructive to both people and organisations. Unfortunately, these are issues that have been around for a long time and will continue until leaders step up and start leading with kindness and compassion.

Kindness is a superpower and a new form of currency for leaders.

Across the pages of history, countless remarkable individuals have illuminated the world with their kind-hearted leadership, leaving a mark of positive change. Malala Yousafzai, the Dalai Lama and Martin Luther King Jr are some of those who stand out. Their kindness had a profound impact as they inspired and helped millions of people all over the world.

We believe that kindness is the new leadership superpower – it's a new and powerful form of currency that can enhance high performance, trust, loyalty and commitment.

Leading with kindness . . .

increases motivation among team members

helps in retaining employees

drives innovation within the team

improves overall performance

boosts the confidence of team members

manifests happiness and well-being in

the workplace

promotes collaboration and teamwork

cultivates open and effective

communication within the team

What Does Leading With Kindness Look Like?

Leading with kindness doesn't mean that there are no boundaries or rules, or that people can fly under the radar. It doesn't mean that the business is a charity, underperformance is accepted or people can hide from their accountabilities. Kindness means that people feel safe and cared for. It means respecting the people you work with, feeling empowered to speak your truth and feeling fulfilled with the work you do. It means that people feel confident to share their voice and challenge the status quo. It means that, when you fall over, someone will be there to pick you up.

We believe that being a kind leader requires courage and strength. Kind leaders are very capable of making good and strong business decisions, even tough decisions, with kindness.

Being a kind leader is essential in today's world as it brings different elements of authenticity, transparency, self-awareness, trust, warmth and emotional intelligence, which are all characteristics and building blocks to being a progressive and successful leader. When we talk about kind leadership, what we really mean is including a little of each of these different attributes in your day-to-day leadership.

Leadership behaviours are changing and so should you. The traditional hierarchical, dictatorship, autocratic leadership style is outdated and no longer effective. It does not allow for employee growth, which is key to building a successful organisation, empowered teams and future leaders. In today's world we need a modern, more contemporary style of leadership.

It's time for kind leaders to step up, have a voice and be the game changers for our generation

> We may not be able to change the past, but we can shape the future.

and future generations. It's time to shine the spotlight on leading with kindness in every aspect of our lives. It's time to change the leadership rules. It's time to challenge the status quo. It's time to embrace a new contemporary style of leadership, and it starts with all of us bringing kindness into our own lives.

Six traits of kind leaders

Compassion

Integrity

Gratitude

Authenticity

Humility

Humour

Model Kind Behaviour

A huge part of being a great leader is understanding and valuing the people you lead. It's about embracing the different personalities you work with and creating a culture that encourages individuals to bring their best selves to work each day (see Chapter 7). Employees want more consistent feedback, delivered with kindness; they want to build trust within their peer group, develop meaningful relationships and have a better 'life in balance' (see page 274).

The role of a leader is to create a 'circle of trust' for their employees – a space where people feel safe, confident to speak up and bring new thinking and ideas to the table. It means having clear expectations, setting boundaries and providing honest, open feedback. When leaders create a circle of trust, people feel supported, connected and fulfilled, and give more of themselves to advance the vision of the organisation.

In our experience, organisations that value kindness have higher employee engagement, lower turnover and higher productivity. Kindness empowers others to lead with positivity, purpose and an open mind. This encourages new ideas, innovation and collaboration. Leading with kindness accelerates trust and loyalty, and, in turn, creates inspired and empowered employees who will go above and beyond to deliver on the organisation's goals and vision.

Great leaders don't have one persona in their personal life and a different one in their professional worlds: great leaders show up as their whole authentic selves always.

Kind leadership for lifelong impact

▲ Set clear expectations.

▲ Give honest feedback.

▲ Lead by example.

▲ Empower others.

▲ Create a safe environment.

▲ Value ideas.

▲ Push beyond comfort zones.

▲ Build connections.

▲ Ask for and give respect.

▲ Support well-being of others.

Five Things Kind Leaders Have in Common

1. Emotional intelligence

Emotional intelligence, also known as EQ, is a topic that has gained traction in recent years and is now considered one of the most critical leadership skills. Research has shown that emotional intelligence is one of the strongest predictors of performance, with around 90 per cent of top performers exhibiting high levels of emotional intelligence.

People with high emotional intelligence are more self-aware, understand themselves at a much deeper level, are better at regulating their actions and controlling their reactions, and are more empathetic. They are also connected to their emotions and, when we are better connected to our emotions, we can better relate to others. People with high emotional intelligence also have a high level of social awareness and the ability to accurately pick up on the emotions of other people.

Emotionally intelligent leaders focus on their health and well-being, practise gratitude and create balance in their lives as they know that they can't achieve their goals unless they're healthy and happy. They can also better manage stress, build trust and maintain healthier relationships.

How to lead with emotional intelligence

- ▲ Be self-aware: Understand and acknowledge your emotions, strengths and weaknesses.
- ▲ Nurture relationships: Listen, empathise and communicate openly.
- ▲ Prioritise well-being: Take care of your physical and mental health.
- ▲ Build trust: Act with integrity and follow through on commitments.
- ▲ Practise gratitude: Appreciate and express thanks.
- ▲ Regulate your actions: Think before you act, considering the impact.

2. Empathy

Empathetic leadership means having the ability to identify with others, understand their points of view, provide appropriate support and be aware of people's feelings and thoughts. Unfortunately, it has long been a soft skill that gets overlooked as a performance indicator.

Empathetic leaders take a genuine interest in the people around them, what inspires them and makes them tick. They are perceptive and show people that they are seen, appreciated, acknowledged and understood.

Being able to demonstrate empathy increases trust, communication and a sense of belonging and worth. Trust creates empowering and honest relationships among teams and the organisation. In turn, this increases collaboration and productivity and, very importantly, demonstrates a culture of care. Without empathy, people feel unsafe, alienated and demotivated.

How to lead with empathy

- ▲ Show interest in others: Demonstrate genuine curiosity about their experiences.
- ▲ Build trust: Be consistent, transparent and reliable.
- ▲ Create a positive environment: Cultivate a supportive and inclusive culture.
- ▲ Be transparent: Share information openly and honestly.
- ▲ Encourage two-way communication: Foster open dialogue and feedback.
- ▲ Provide support: Offer assistance and guidance when needed.

3. A people-first mindset

A people-first mindset is all about investing in your employees – in their happiness, in their employee experience and in their growth. When you invest in your team in this way, they're going to be more engaged with their work and the organisation.

Kind leaders with a people-first mindset think about how their people want to work, what motivates them and what inspires them. They prioritise employees' health and well-being, show genuine care and invite employee feedback. They push employees outside their comfort zone, encourage high performance and empower them to be the leader in their roles.

Having a people-first mindset translates to a host of positive outcomes: it boosts employee engagement, retains talent, increases job satisfaction and productivity, builds connection, and improves top-line revenue and bottom-line profits.

How to lead with a people-first mindset

- ▲ Invest in people: Develop and support your team members.
- ▲ Prioritise well-being: Promote a healthy 'life in balance'.
- ▲ Encourage high performance: Set clear expectations and recognise achievements.
- ▲ Empower leadership: Delegate authority and offer leadership opportunities.
- ▲ Empower others to lead: Encourage leadership development and mentorship.
- ▲ Push comfort zones: Challenge individuals with new and stretching assignments.

4. Self-awareness

Self-awareness is an admirable trait in leaders because it means that they have the willingness to know themselves and their team members. They have an awareness of how their personality, habits and skills impact and connect with those around them.

Self-awareness requires high emotional intelligence, flexibility, resilience and adaptability. Without self-awareness, you fail to see the patterns in your behaviours and thinking, and struggle to regulate your own feelings.

A leader with self-awareness inspires others by aligning their words with actions and shows self-control, especially when challenged or stressed. They have a conscious understanding of their character, motivate, lead by example and understand how these things impact their leadership behaviour and abilities.

Leaders with high levels of self-awareness actively consider how their actions, words, decisions and reactions are perceived by others. Self-awareness promotes personal growth and control, which enable leaders to leverage their advantages to lead teams to the greatest results.

By reaching this point in the book, you have already made significant progress on your journey of self-awareness. The steps you have taken and the insights you have gained demonstrate your commitment to elevating your life. Your dedication to exploring and understanding yourself is paving the way for building a strong foundation for future success.

How to lead with self-awareness

- ▲ Make better decisions: Recognise biases and emotions.
- ▲ Encourage feedback: Seek input for growth.
- ▲ Set boundaries: Protect time and well-being.
- ▲ Set goals: Align with values for growth.
- ▲ Be mindful of actions: Take responsibility for choices.
- ▲ Adapt to change: Embrace flexibility and resilience.

5. Humility

Humble leaders make the best leaders. This statement is not something we are just claiming to be true. In Jim Collins' book *Good to Great*, he shares extensive research data on how humble and wilful leaders help their organisations grow and sustain market position.

Humble leaders understand that leadership is all about working for the greater good and being in service to others. They lead to transform, take responsibility when things don't go to plan, and are quick to acknowledge the work and efforts of others when things turn out well.

They give everyone the opportunity to contribute and share their views. This encourages people to share their voice, take risks and put forward ideas, which improves company productivity, performance and the bottom line.

How to lead with humility

- ▲ **Be humble:** Embrace humility and value others' contributions.
- ▲ **Share the credit:** Recognise and acknowledge your team's achievements.
- ▲ **Serve others:** Prioritise the well-being and growth of your team.
- ▲ **Lead to transform:** Inspire positive change and growth.
- ▲ **Encourage sharing:** Foster open communication and idea sharing.
- ▲ **Support risk-taking:** Create an environment that encourages innovation.

Take action

From the lists in this section, choose how you will upgrade your behaviour and lead with kindness.

- ▲ What can you stop, start and keep?
- ▲ How can you elevate?

Unlocking Kindness

Kindness can apply to so many areas of our lives: our workplace, relationships and our personal lives such as with our children, family and friends, in our schools, and within our communities.

Answer the following questions to unlock the high performance kindness in all areas of your life:

- ▲ What does kind leadership mean to you?
- ▲ What two acts of kindness could you undertake in the workplace or at home today?
- ▲ Are you able to forgive others for their mistakes?
- ▲ Are you able to maintain respectful dialogue with someone who strongly disagrees with you?
- ▲ When you make a mistake, do you take responsibility?
- ▲ Are you happy for others when they succeed?
- ▲ How do you generally deliver feedback?
- ▲ When negative emotions arise, how do you deal with them?
- ▲ How could you offer feedback to your team in a way that makes them feel supported?

To be more connected, what are some of the qualities you need to work on yourself?

It's time to shine the spotlight on leading and living with kindness in all areas of our lives.

Imagine a word filled with kindness!

Colleen: Kindness is at the heart of how I lead. I believe it's a precious gift we can offer others. As a leader, my mission has been to create workplaces where people thrive and find purpose beyond their roles. I genuinely connect with my team, understand their aspirations and provide unwavering support. I believe that when we prioritise their well-being and growth, they reciprocate by caring for the organisation. People are the driving force, so treating them with kindness is imperative.

By nurturing a culture of kindness, we unlock each individual's potential and create an environment where everyone can thrive. Kindness is not just a value; it's the guiding principle that shapes my leadership. It fosters genuine flourishing, effective collaboration and organisational success.

Kindness summary

1. Kindness is a superpower and it's a new and powerful form of currency that can enhance high performance, trust, loyalty and commitment.
2. Kindness is a strength, not a weakness.
3. The six attributes you need to upgrade living and leading with kindness are: compassion, integrity, gratitude, authenticity, humility and humour.
4. Bringing kindness into your life and leadership starts with being kind to yourself.
5. A culture of kindness leads to happier, more harmonious and productive teams.

Create Your Personal High-Performance Plan: KINDNESS

Using the list on page 210, write three things you can implement to upgrade your kindness:

1. _____
2. _____
3. _____

To elevate kindness:

What do you need to STOP doing?

1. _____
   _____
2. _____
   _____
3. _____
   _____

What do you need to START doing?

1. _____
   _____
2. _____
   _____
3. _____
   _____

What do you need to KEEP doing?

1. _____
   _____
2. _____
   _____
3. _____
   _____

Chapter 11

Set Your Goals

My goal is not to be better than anyone else, but to be better than I used to be

WAYNE DYER

oal-setting is the fundamental key to success, defining the pathway to your elevated future.

Hard-hitting goals get world-class results. They are full of fuel and, with exceptional commitment, reward you with results that fast-track you to showing up as a strong, confident and courageous human being and leader. Sharpening your focus and awareness on your leadership journey with a base of solid values, a clear vision, hard-hitting goals and a growth mindset will allow you to lead yourself and others with energy and purpose, and achieve great success. It is not about doing more, it is about simplifying and sharpening your focus to get great results.

Goal-setting is a powerful process to master to maintain your focus, sustain motivation and confirm daily purpose as you bring your vision to life. Stretch goals propel us beyond our comfort zones, unlocking untapped potential and paving the way for extraordinary achievements.

The process of setting goals helps you identify where you want to go in life and the steps you need to take to get there. Knowing precisely what you want to achieve allows you to concentrate all your efforts and actions into the right areas with simple choices.

Goals are dreams with deadlines.

Tony Robbins states, 'When you set a goal, your brain evaluates its emotional significance and the effort required. It gives priority to goals with high emotional significance, proving that "where focus goes, energy flows".'

Goal-setting is an essential personal leadership skill and is fundamental to leading others. Whether you are a solo-operator, entrepreneur, manager of a small team or a CEO, goal-setting is one of the most effective skills to conquer for greatness.

Master the Basics First

Watching and working with high-performance athletes and great leaders we have seen first-hand the power of goal-setting. But when we speak at conferences and personally work with clients, we are always amazed at how many people don't commit to the basics.

Take action

Ask yourself the following questions:

▲ Do you have goals?

▲ Are they written down?

▲ Are they somewhere you see them every day?

▲ Have you shared them with people you trust who will support you and keep you accountable?

Usually, when we ask the above questions during our courses, only a small handful of people can honestly put their hand up. High performers who love success, achievement and results, have purpose and passion, and know how to set goals effectively are few and far between. They fully commit to the basic four fundamentals of goal-setting as outlined opposite. How would your life and leadership capability change if you mastered these basics?

The four fundamentals of goal-setting

1. **Focus:** Where your focus goes your energy flows. Goals breed focus.
2. **Measurement:** What gets measured gets improved. As you measure you have a basis on which to improve. Goals are to be measured.
3. **Alignment:** Personal greatness comes from goals aligned with your values and the leader you want to be. Goals keep you on the right track.
4. **Inspiration:** Goals breathe life into your days. Setting goals is a statement that you refuse to be ordinary. It is a bold play for your best life. Goals challenge the brain.

High performers set regular goals that are fully focused on what they want to achieve, how they want to feel in the process and how they want to show up and perform to get the results they crave. It is their most valuable tool and something they can fully own. It gives them clear direction and focus on what to do, how to do it and when to do it, ensuring they spend their energy on the most important and prioritised tasks.

Goals provide the motivational energy to carry on, even when motivation is low.

Take action

▲ **Maintain clear focus on your goals:** Clearly define your objectives, ensuring they are specific, measurable, attainable, relevant and time-bound (SMART), to keep your attention directed towards what you want to achieve.

▲ **Employ effective measurement techniques:** Break down your goals into smaller, manageable tasks, establish measurable indicators and set deadlines and milestones that align with your overall objective, enabling you to track progress and ensure accountability.

▲ **Ensure alignment with your vision and values:** Regularly review and monitor your progress, making necessary adjustments along the way to stay aligned with your larger goals and to maintain consistency with your core values and long-term vision.

▲ **Seek inspiration and support:** Share your goals with trusted individuals who can offer guidance and support, and hold you accountable. Celebrate milestones and accomplishments, leveraging them as sources of inspiration to fuel motivation and maintain a positive mindset throughout your journey.

The athlete's way

Athletes set goals with specific results for competition: performance goals to support them to adjust and make improvements over the training periods; and process goals which direct their concentration when carrying out a specific skill and blocking out competition and crowds. Outcome goals, on the other hand, provide athletes with a clear target to strive for, often focusing on the end result they desire, such as winning a championship or achieving a personal record, serving as a source of motivation and inspiration throughout their training and competition.

Try it when setting your own goals:

▲ **Outcome goals:** These focus on the end result or outcome you desire to achieve, such as winning a competition, obtaining a specific promotion or reaching a certain income level. They provide a clear target to strive for and can be highly motivating.

▲ **Performance goals:** These centre around improving your personal performance and skills. They involve setting specific targets for enhancing your abilities, such as increasing your sales numbers, improving your athletic speed or enhancing your public speaking skills.

▲ **Process goals:** These concentrate on the specific actions, behaviours or processes you need to engage in to achieve your desired outcome or performance goals. They break down the larger goal into manageable steps and focus on the actions within your control, such as practising for a certain number of hours each day, following a specific study routine or consistently networking with industry professionals. Process goals help build consistency and develop the necessary habits for success.

High-Performance Personal Goal-Setting

Once you have mastered the basics of goal-setting, follow these tips to elevate your goals and success in your career and personal life. Remember, world-class performance is in the detail.

Pick with passion

Your goals should be those things that really matter and are meaningful to you, and make you feel passionate and proud once you achieve them.

Take time to really think

Get clear on your why. Take time to think what you want more of, what you want less of and what you genuinely enjoy in your personal and professional life.

Look at past successes

Learn from the past as both success and failure leave valuable clues. What skill sets did you use; what worked and what didn't? What was important about the goals? What has changed since then?

Express yourself positively

State each goal as a positive statement that is reflective of the outcome you want for yourself. Get into a high-performance mindset: 'I will enhance my professional skills by completing an online course in my field by the end of the year and earn a certificate, and I will expand my network and build meaningful connections by attending at least two industry conferences or networking events each financial year.'

Set priorities

You will often have several goals which can take time to accomplish. Therefore, you should prioritise your goals in order of importance, so you are focused on what really matters most.

Share your goals

It's easier to hold yourself accountable to your goals if others know about them. Tell a positive and supportive friend, a family member or a colleague and provide updates on your progress. Beware of dream-stealers and share only with your trusted 'I believe in you' group. This also gives you someone to celebrate with when you accomplish your goals.

Hold yourself accountable

Embrace visibility as you set your goal and throughout the process of achieving it. Establish check-in points to monitor your progress, celebrate milestones and reward yourself along the way.

Visualise your goals

Picture yourself achieving the goal and think about the benefits it'll provide you when you conquer it. This will keep you motivated and positive, and give you the push you need to get across the finish line.

Celebrate your victories

Celebrating small wins triggers feelings of happiness and pride, breeding further inner self-confidence (see page 365). This keeps you inspired as you reflect on your wins, sit in and experience the feelings, and express gratitude for those who supported you, and is fundamental in staying motivated towards your big-picture goals. Remember success is best when it's shared.

Write them down

Write down your goals somewhere you'll regularly see them. This makes them feel real, helps you remember them and is a constant reminder to get to work. Don't write them on a computer in a file somewhere deep in the depths of your Dropbox – put them on paper or in a journal. Write down why they are important and the details of how they will make you feel when achieved.

> Goals must be written: Goals must be seen.

Take action

▲ What is most important to you right now?
▲ What lessons have you learnt from past successes?
▲ When will you schedule your check-in points?
▲ What do you feel when you visualise yourself smashing the goal?
▲ How will you celebrate?

We achieve more when we write down our goals and back them up with actions. Without action, nothing happens. So, take the time to find clarity, get the words right, feel them, engage with them and then share them. And ask yourself, out loud, does this goal warm your heart, spark your energy and serve your vision, values and how you want to feel and show up and lead in the world?

Think it, define it, write it. Set the goal. Then take action.

Fifty small goals to kick-start your elevated high-performance life

Life passes us by quickly, and it's within our power to make each year remarkable.

Take inspiration from these tips to live without regrets:

1. Plan and organise your weekly schedule.
2. Stay active every day.
3. Cultivate a strong sense of gratitude.
4. Strive for improvement in your work daily.
5. Seek guidance from a mentor.
6. Identify the most important priorities in your life.
7. Define and express your unique identity.
8. Explore art galleries for inspiration.
9. Connect with nature through walks in the bush.
10. Practise forgiveness and inner peace.
11. Keep a journal to capture your thoughts.
12. Say no to distractions that hinder your focus.
13. Maintain a balanced and healthy diet.
14. Extend your support to others.
15. Express gratitude with thank-you letters.
16. Discover new role models.
17. Cultivate patience and compassion.
18. Cherish unforgettable moments with loved ones.
19. Exhibit genuine politeness and kindness.
20. Stay true to your authentic self.
21. Envision a meaningful direction for your life.
22. Enjoy the uplifting power of music.
23. Pursue your passions and follow your dreams.
24. Infuse passion into everything you do.
25. Recognise and leverage your unique strengths.

26. Collaborate and be a supportive team player.
27. Explore new places and experiences.
28. Take responsibility for your mistakes.
29. Lead your own life with purpose and intention.
30. Celebrate others' achievements.
31. Be present.
32. Embrace contentment with what you have.
33. Embrace innovation and continuous improvement.
34. Don't let critics drain your energy.
35. Read regularly to expand your knowledge.
36. Make your life one of impact.
37. Strive to be the best version of yourself.
38. Start each day with positive self-talk.
39. Embrace self-care.
40. Take three deep breaths to start your day.
41. Cultivate a daily mindfulness practice.
42. Embrace change as a pathway to growth.
43. Engage in frequent acts of goodwill.
44. Set aside time for creative expression.
45. Challenge yourself to learn new skills.
46. Practise empathy and active listening.
47. Volunteer and give back to your community.
48. Embrace solitude for self-reflection.
49. Cultivate a sense of wonder and curiosity.
50. Set clear boundaries to protect your well-being.

Professional Goal-Setting

Professional goals are goalposts for what you personally want to achieve and where you want to go in your career. To elevate, they can be short term, which are more tactical and help you today or this year, or they can be more strategic in their nature and guide your long-term career aspirations.

There are two main areas for long-term career goal-setting:

1. **Planning your next career move:** Where do you see yourself in five years' time? What do you want to achieve in the company you are in, where do you want to go?
2. **Planning your transition or retirement:** What do you want to do next? How can you make an impact? What legacy do you want to leave? How do you want to spend your retirement years?

Goal-setting helps leaders stay focused on what truly matters, lead the team and bring the company vision to life. These goals direct everyday tasks and prioritise whether they are urgent or important.

There is no one responsible for leaders, so making sure they are motivated and truly committed to the job comes back to them. As a leader or coach, you are also responsible for your employees' motivation and engagement too.

There are not a lot of true and authentic leaders in our society, but studying leaders from the past, who led by example, who inspired you, who you trusted, who were loyal, had integrity and remained humble, open-minded and made a difference gives you clues. You can model your own leadership journey from those clues.

Examples of high-performance career goals

Develop executive presence: Your ability to lead a group, measured by their likelihood to follow you and your direction, and positively viewed across the wider team.

Communicate with influence and impact: The most effective communicators clearly inform teams and actively listen to them at the same time. They can communicate in an inclusive way which involves positive connection with others.

Effectively manage through conflict: Team conflict impacts both the mental and emotional well-being of employees. It has a severe cost, leading to stress, high levels of absenteeism and low levels of employee engagement. Learning to have difficult conversations, approaching all individuals in the team personally, focusing on relationships, creating a plan, following up and getting external support is a part of high-performance leadership.

Provide effective feedback: Doing this right is the gift you give to others. Constructive feedback enriches relationships and brings the team's performance to an elevated level. Mastering the COIN framework – context, observation, impact, next (see box opposite) – will elevate your feedback success and make both positive and constructive feedback more impactful.

The COIN framework

The COIN framework, developed by Anna Carroll, is a structured approach used for providing feedback or reflecting on experiences:

▲ **Context:** This involves providing the necessary background information and setting the stage for feedback or reflection. It helps to establish the context and specific circumstances surrounding the situation being discussed.

▲ **Observation:** This step focuses on describing the specific behaviours or actions that were observed during the situation. It entails providing objective and specific details about what occurred without judgement or interpretation.

▲ **Impact:** This step addresses the consequences or effects of the observed behaviours or actions. It explores how these behaviours or actions affected individuals or the overall outcome of the situation. This can include both positive and negative impacts.

▲ **Next:** The final step involves discussing the next steps or actions that can be taken to improve or build upon the observed behaviours or actions. It emphasises constructive suggestions, recommendations or areas for development based on the context, observation and impact discussed earlier.

The COIN formula provides a framework to structure feedback or reflection conversations, enabling clear communication and a focus on improvement and growth.

Efficiently and effectively navigate uncertainty: Developing your own resilience and leveraging your own strengths and the strengths of those in the team will lead to your ability to embrace and navigate change, transformation and uncertain times.

Sharpen time-management skills: The most common professional goal is gaining control of their calendar. Sharpening this skill involves gracious communication and collaboration with others, delegation, prioritisation and self-awareness to how you perform at your best. Clear, confident boundaries are a fundamental of time management.

Develop inclusive leadership and teams: There are six behaviour traits to develop as an inclusive leader: relationship-building, recognition, empathy, social connection, encouragement of participation and alignment. Developing inclusive leadership and teams fosters a culture of diversity and belonging, leading to increased collaboration, innovation and employee engagement (see page 199 for more on this).

Upskill with a professional certificate or degree: Continuing your education via online or in-person courses, while working or taking a sabbatical, broadens your perspectives and keeps you relevant as your skills improve. Never stop learning.

Expand network: Having a wide, strong, well-developed and nurtured network is the greatest way to catapult your career growth and opens up the door for high-performance mentorship. Attending conferences, workshops, joining network groups and connecting with people via social media channels so you can meet and learn from others is a powerful goal to set for both the short and long term.

Be intentional with self-care: An essential part of high performance is the ability to manage stress and avoid burnout. Protection of your mental, physical, emotional and spiritual health is a goal for long-term sustainability at a high level.

Dealing with setbacks

No road to a goal that is epic and worth fighting for is a smooth and paved rosy experience. Goal-setting is a continuous long-term process that requires constant updating and fine-tuning, but through the habit of goal-setting you can nurture the big-picture dream, pivot quickly when necessary, keep your passion burning, keep persistent and keep pushing through.

A true leader and high-performing individual often strives for perfection while realising it is impossible to attain. They do not let perfection get in the way of progress. As such, they build in the expectation to fail often and simply factor losses into the equation. A solid leader can own and move beyond their mistakes and failures gracefully, and empower others to do the same.

Eight top tactics for high-performance success

1. Conduct a daily goal review.
2. Cultivate a complaint-free mindset.
3. Eliminate distractions and tidy up loose ends.
4. Break down daunting tasks into manageable steps.
5. Envision where you will be and how you will feel on 31 December – visualise your desired outcome.
6. Organise your work into 90-day thematic cycles.
7. Engage in business networking to expand your connections and foster accountability.
8. Continuously strive to outlearn and surpass your previous self each year.

Goal-setting is your statement that you refuse to be ordinary.

Shannah: I have spent over twenty years around high-performance athletes and their coaches and have coached many high performers in my private coaching business. I feel incredibly privileged to have had such a close view, to observe what did and didn't work, and to witness people reach their dreams and goals. I've also seen high performers pivot as some had obstacles too big to overcome but reset their goals and kept powering on to achieve world-class success.

I have built a solid business on referral only, conquered the fear of speaking in public and written seven books, and each time have set the goal, written it down, blocked out the time and put in pure focus to finish the project. I have applied this to everything in life – everything is written, recorded, shared, celebrated and all of it has given me the gift of a life I love, which is not perfect but is full of clarity, purpose and direction, and incredible experiences, both big and small.

I may get curveballs, but they are what make life interesting and challenge me outside my comfort zone. I am flowing and embracing change, learning that there is a grey zone sometimes and not everything is black or white. I am committed to showing up, open-hearted, doing my best and confirming 'I've got this' as a part of my existence.

Goal-setting summary

1. Hard-hitting goals get results.
2. Goals must be written down.
3. Goals need actions that can start immediately.
4. A high-performance leader can build resilience in the face of change, hardship and knockbacks.
5. Celebration is a key part of high-performance long-term motivation.

Create Your Personal High-Performance Plan: GOAL-SETTING

Write down your top three goals:

1. _____
2. _____
3. _____

To elevate your goals:

What do you need to STOP doing?

1. _____
_____
2. _____
_____
3. _____
_____

What do you need to START doing?

1. _____
_____
2. _____
_____
3. _____
_____

What do you need to KEEP doing?

1. _____
_____
2. _____
_____
3. _____

Chapter 12

Create Your Habit Plan

Success isn't always about greatness. It's about consistency. Consistent hard work leads to success. Greatness will come

DWAYNE JOHNSON

abits are the cornerstone of day-to-day living. Sixty per cent of actions people take each day are not actual decisions but rather habits playing out subconsciously.

For better or worse, your habits shape you, define you and are the daily building blocks to success. Habits are thoughts and behaviours so strongly wired into your mind that you perform them without thinking. Just like brushing your teeth and driving your car, you don't have to think how to do them, you just do them. Habits become ingrained through repetition over time, making them hard to break or change. But successful people form habits that feed their success, rather than their failure. They do what it takes to get the job done. They own their habits, work with them, master them and consistently review them.

The ultimate purpose of a habit is to solve a problem in life with as little energy as possible. Your identity emerges from your habits as every action you take is forming the type of person you wish to become. But habits are a two-edged sword. They can both benefit and disadvantage you, so it's important to understand them.

To elevate in any area of your life, a big bright spotlight needs to be shone on the tiny habits that make up your moments, which in turn make up your days, which in turn make up the story of your life.

What matters most is asking whether your current habits are putting you on the path to success. Your fitness is a result of your exercise habits or lack of; your knowledge is a result of your learning habits or lack of. At the end of the day, we get what we repeat.

Just because you always have a glass of wine as a habit when you get home from work, doesn't mean it is a good habit leading to peak health. You could fine-tune it to have two glasses of water when you get home from work and go for a walk around the block, then see if you want the glass of wine depending on your health goals. You park your car at work and rush in to start the day; instead, fine-tune your state of mind and take three deep breaths, gather yourself, set your intention and then walk into the office.

It is a habit to be kind, it is a habit to hydrate, it is a habit to say thank you, it is a habit to look in the mirror, it is a habit to do breathwork, it is a habit to brush your teeth, it is a habit to walk every day, it is a habit to write your goals, your journal and your gratitude.

Supercharged habits are simple, productive actions, repeated consistently over time that will fuel your fire.

Small Changes Make a Big Difference

Sometimes we get swept up in the thought that massive success requires massive action, but that's not sustainable. You may want to pay off your mortgage, write a book, win a championship, build great wealth or overhaul your body image and level of health and well-being, or you may want to make earth-shattering change and get people talking. It rarely works. The vision and goal may be there, but the tiny powerful habits are not. That is why diets don't work long term, gym memberships lapse and New Year's resolutions don't come to fruition – the habits are not tuned properly.

The secret to getting great results in life is to never stop making small 1 per cent improvements, making ten just slight, conscious tweaks a day, or more. Always look for the next way to get 1 per cent better: what time you get up, what, when and how you eat, what you drink, your sleep hygiene, your relationships, your exercise, your spending and saving, your connection levels, your friendship and network circles, your learning, your leadership skills – everything compounds in one direction or another.

To upgrade and master your habits, begin by identifying what is and isn't working for you. Almost everything you do you can do a little better – you have the opportunity to elevate 1 per cent each and every day. Set up effective systems that support your goals, shift your mindset to embrace growth and seek account-ability to stay on track. Every action you take has an impact not only on your own life but also on the lives of those around you, including loved ones, friends and co-workers. By striving for personal excellence, you create a ripple effect that can elevate the experiences and interactions you share with others, leaving a lasting positive influence.

The choice is simple, and it is yours to make every hour, every day. Your habits are the only things standing between you and the success you want in your incredible and precious life.

Take action

▲ Have you spent a lot of time working on your habits or has life happened too fast and you just went with it?

▲ What are your habits?

▲ Are they getting the results you want?

▲ What comes first in line to stop, start or keep from your daily program?

Master the Basics of High-Performance Leadership Habits

To become great, to feel how you want to feel, to move how you want to with strength and flexibility, to have fulfilling, meaningful and soul-nourishing relationships and to handle change, some high-performance skills need to be adopted. Get clear on what you really want and what habits will produce the result.

'Mastery' is the process of building up your knowledge or skills in a focused area, which can then form the basis for further development and new habits. Each habit continues to unlock the next level of performance. The cycle is endless. The cycle is exciting. The cycle can create magical results.

Over the course of our careers, we have observed five transformative habits that contribute to success and personal growth:

1. **Take proactive ownership:** Focus on what you can control and influence, taking action to create positive change.
2. **Envision your desired outcomes:** Set clear measures of success and create a plan to achieve your goals.
3. **Prioritise what truly matters:** Focus on your most important goals and tasks, avoiding constant reactivity to urgencies.
4. **Foster a mindset of mutual success:** Nurture an environment of collaboration and trust by striving for outcomes that benefit all parties involved.
5. **Prioritise understanding others:** Positively influence and connect with individuals by cultivating empathy, actively listening to their needs and seeking to comprehend their viewpoints before sharing your own.

By embracing these habits consistently, you can elevate your performance, enhance your relationships and lead a more purposeful and fulfilling life. These principles, inspired by timeless wisdom, have the power to transform your journey towards success and personal fulfilment.

Shining a light on your habits is a high-performance continuous process. There is no finish line as life keeps changing, so your habits must be modified.

Olympic athletes, actors, businesspeople and other high performers engage in regular reviews and reflections to improve their performance. It's not enough to learn and adopt new habits; it's crucial to regularly fine-tune them. Just like tuning a guitar, a tennis racquet or a car engine for optimal performance, constant attention is required for sustained high performance.

As leadership starts with self, how you start, pace and finish your day will be determined by the structures, habits, rituals and routines you create, commit to and constantly tune.

Take action

▲ What went well in the past six months?

▲ What didn't go so well in the past six months?

▲ What did you learn?

▲ What can you stop, start and keep now?

Habit stacking

Habit linking, or stacking, involves creating straightforward, repeatable sequences (guided by a checklist) to accomplish more within a condensed timeframe. This approach prevents excessive thinking, as you only need to follow the checklist rather than concentrating on each distinct habit. You can start to habit-stack by consistently executing the same sequence of actions in the same way each day. Checklists not only offer guidance, but also help to cut down complexity and enhance effectiveness. Instead of coupling your new habit with a fresh timeframe and location, you integrate it into an existing routine.

Habits + deliberate practice + continuous improvement + stacking = next-level performance and self-mastery.

Habit stacking is a simple technique for forming new habits:

1. Select a new habit you wish to incorporate into your routine.
2. Identify an existing daily activity that can serve as an anchor for the new habit.
3. Link the new habit to the existing activity by performing them together.
4. Repeat the habit stack consistently until it becomes automatic in your daily life.

Examples of habit stacking

▲ After you turn off your alarm in the morning, you drink a cup of water.

▲ After you brush your teeth in the morning, you walk for an hour.

▲ After you shower, you high-five yourself in the mirror.

▲ After you wash your hands, you take three deep grounding breaths.

▲ After you sit at your desk, you say your affirmation for the day.

▲ After you eat dinner, you prepare your food for the following day.

▲ After you tidy the kitchen, you brush your teeth.

▲ After you brush your teeth, you stretch in front of the TV before sitting on the couch.

▲ After you get into bed at night, you journal for five minutes.

▲ After you read, you kiss your partner goodnight.

The stacked habits you perform every day will become an automatic part of your routine.

Let's start with defining your basic habit stacks on how you start, lead and finish your day. Do you just get up for work, go for a walk, get to work, survive the day, come home to the chores and dinner and then hit the couch? How can you elevate this whole experience?

Start first with your bookends of the day – how you start and finish the day – which are generally more within your control, then progress into habits you can control when the world opens up and outside influences come in. Focus here on what you can control. This is your life and your time. We all have seventy-two blocks of twenty minutes to spend and experience each day – so use your minutes well.

Make the most of your minutes; they make up the story of your life.

- ▲ It only takes a minute to face a fear head-on.
- ▲ It only takes a minute to say thank you.
- ▲ It only takes a minute to say your affirmation.
- ▲ It only takes a minute to read an amazing idea that might really excite you.
- ▲ It only takes a minute to set a goal.
- ▲ It only takes a minute to go above and beyond at work.
- ▲ It only takes a minute to reflect on how you can improve each day.
- ▲ It only takes a minute to connect with a friend or colleague.
- ▲ It only takes a minute to help someone who needs it.
- ▲ It only takes a minute to change your life for the better.

Make Your Own High-Performance Habit Plan

We watch a very distinct set of habits on display when we view sport. We watch the athlete warm up with a very specific routine, we enjoy the match watching their goals come to life – their values, habits, behaviours, mindset, confidence levels, personal brand and team culture unfold before our eyes. We then watch as they have very specific routines and habits on how to cool down and recover to perform again the next day.

To elevate your own personal daily experience, a starting point is to view yourself as an athlete competing in a marathon each day. A day in our life is akin to running a marathon, where we must warm up by setting intentions and preparing ourselves mentally and physically, embrace the pace of the day by staying focused and present, and then cool down by reflecting, unwinding and preparing for restorative sleep.

Take action

▲ Define and write down how you will prepare and warm up for the race of the day (your career).

▲ Decide how you will pace the day like an athlete with fuelling stops.

▲ Note down how you will recover properly from the day so you can get up with enthusiasm and energy to do it all again tomorrow.

Life is a marathon		Ideas to elevate	Habits to establish
Morning	Prepare for the race	▲ Take three conscious breaths as you wake ▲ Make your bed + put on exercise clothes ▲ Move your body + stretch ▲ Mindfully breathe + say affirmations ▲ Mirror work (see page 105) + shower + mindfully feel the water ▲ Meditation + journal + healthy breakfast	
Day	Pace the race	▲ Drive to work + listen to podcast ▲ Connect with your goals + state your affirmations ▲ Set limits on meetings/calls ▲ Do the most important tasks first (see page 10) ▲ No caffeine after 1 pm ▲ Shutdown ritual: prepare for tomorrow	
Evening	Recovery from race	▲ Set time for tech turn-off ▲ Journal + reflect on the day + meditate ▲ Read ten pages of a book every night ▲ Put out exercise clothes before going to bed ▲ Gratitude journal before turning off light ▲ Three conscious breaths as you go to sleep	

The top five habits of high-performance leadership

Today's workplace demands have risen post pandemic, and the landscape has changed significantly to a hybrid workplace. It is essential with these working arrangements that leaders at all levels can build habits that foster strong relationships and motivate employees to perform at their best.

So, what behaviours of successful leaders can you include in your plan?

1. **Connect team and personal work to the company's values, vision and goals:** They make sure their work goals match the team's goals and the company's overall mission. They often think about the bigger picture.

2. **Share thoughts, ideas and plans effectively:** They're good at choosing the best way to speak based on the situation, and they explain things clearly and simply. They always come prepared. They often adjust how they talk to lead everyone well.

3. **Give team members what they need to succeed:** Leaders use what they know to make quick decisions and help others do the same. They adapt how they work to make sure everyone has what they need to perform well. They're good at making fast decisions about what's required.

4. **Lift individual performance by understanding emotions and how best to work with employees:** They build safe and trusting relationships with their team and get great results together. They have regular meetings with their team members, talk clearly, give helpful advice, and praise people for doing well.

5. **Support others to do better with feedback, guidance and support:** Successful leaders use their knowledge and experience to help and lift up others. They spend time coaching and guiding people, no matter how well they're doing. They're good at mentoring and elevating others.

Habits. They are small. They are powerful. They pack a punch. They are your secret weapon to leading a stellar life. They will make you or break you. Get in touch with them and make sure they are working for you, giving you the results you want in all areas of your life and leadership journey. Eliminate the habits that trip you up, uncover the roots of your habits, swap out bad habits for good ones, one at a time, and build in intrinsic motivation – know your why. Get clear on the actions you need to take to make change, to upgrade, to elevate your life, your leadership journey and ultimately your longevity in life.

Leadership starts with leading yourself. Change your habits, change your life.

Colleen: Habits support and bring my goals and vision to life, and breed intention and high performance into everything I do. Creating great habits supports me to live in line with my values as my values are how I make decisions and are also centred around the things that are most important in the way I live and work.

Building strong and sustainable habits into my life and leadership allows me to have a positive and growth mindset and supports me to build confidence because I am prioritising my health and well-being, setting clear goals and boundaries, and making myself the asset.

Creating 'bookends' to my day has been part of my habit stacking for a very long time and allows me to start the day with purpose and clarity and end the day feeling fulfilled and grateful. My morning habit is to move my body, mindfully breathe and make my bed . . . the '3Ms'. My night routine is to write in my journal, shower before bed and always be in bed by 10 pm. These habits not only allow me to conquer my day but also help me sleep well at night.

Habits summary

1. First we make our habits and then our habits make us.
2. Reflection and review of tiny habits is a high-performance skill.
3. Habit stacking will fast-track you to success.
4. Habits have a compounding effect for big results.
5. Master your own habit plan, starting with how you start and finish your day.

Create Your Personal High-Performance Plan: HABITS

Take a look at your habits:

▲ Are they working for you?
▲ Are they elevating you to new heights?
▲ Have you challenged them?
▲ Can you do 1 per cent better?

To elevate your habits:

What do you need to STOP doing?

1. _____
   _____
2. _____
   _____
3. _____
   _____

What do you need to START doing?

1. _____
   _____
2. _____
   _____
3. _____
   _____

What do you need to KEEP doing?

1. _____
   _____
2. _____
   _____
3. _____
   _____

Pillar 3

LONGEVITY

Self-Management

Self-management is the cornerstone of longevity. By cultivating the ability to effectively manage ourselves, including our emotions, behaviours and choices, we can create a solid foundation for well-being and resilience. Self-management empowers us to make conscious decisions that align with our values and goals, fostering a sense of purpose and meaning in our actions. It enables us to navigate challenges and setbacks with grace, adapt to change and maintain a healthy life in balance.

Moreover, embracing fulfilment is the key to lasting success in life and ensures that we prioritise what truly matters to us. Rather than chasing external markers of achievement or societal expectations, we shift our focus towards personal growth, joy and meaningful connections. Fulfilment arises from aligning our actions with our passions and values, pursuing activities that bring us joy and fulfilment and nurturing our physical, mental and emotional well-being. By embracing fulfilment as the guiding compass in our lives, we unlock a deeper sense of satisfaction and contentment, leading to a more sustainable and fulfilling journey towards success and longevity.

Chapter 13

Understand and Prevent Burnout

Stress is the body's way of signalling that something needs attention, while burnout is nature's way of telling us to change our approach

ARIANNA HUFFINGTON

Burnout is a state of complete physical, mental and emotional exhaustion that's excessive and prolonged. It occurs when we feel overwhelmed, stressed, emotionally drained and unable to meet constant demands. This feeling can lead to professional dissatisfaction and affect other areas of life, such as your overall contentment, relationships, health and well-being.

Burnout costs our healthcare system billions of dollars every year and endangers the well-being of thousands, many of whom are women. In fact, research shows that more than 75 per cent of Australian and New Zealand workers experienced burnout in 2020 which was above the global average.

The truth is, burnout can happen to anyone, and it doesn't just happen at work. You can get burnt out in all areas of life and leadership, and it doesn't just affect you, it affects the people around you – family, friends and colleagues – because they don't get the best version of you.

Understanding and recognising the symptoms and causes of burnout can provide you with a roadmap to build strategies into your life to prevent it and elevate your life.

What Causes Burnout?

Burnout isn't solely caused by work-related stress, an overpacked schedule, too many meetings in the diary or too many responsibilities. It can be experienced by anyone dealing with chronic stress and pressure in their personal and professional lives.

Work	Personal
Unreasonable time pressures	Attitude of perfectionism
Lack of support from leader	Lack of social support
Lack of clarity in the role	Poor self-scare
Unmanageable workload	People-pleasing
Unfair treatment	Perceived lack of control
Workaholic mentality	Lack of boundaries
Work–life imbalance	Extremes in activity
Unclear job expectations	Prolonged stress
High-pressure work environment	Overpacked schedule

Is it stress or is it burnout?

Too much stress can lead to burnout. But stress and burnout are not the same.

Stress is a normal reaction to everyday pressures and can vary in its impact on our daily functioning. It is the body's response to any change that creates physical, emotional or psychological strain. When we feel under pressure, overwhelmed by a busy schedule or threatened, stress affects our overall well-being and behaviour. It arises in situations where we perceive a lack of control or management.

Definition: Stress is a state of mental or emotional strain or tension that arises from challenging or demanding circumstances. It is a response to adverse situations or pressures that affect our well-being.

Stress involves the activation of two systems in our body: the sympathetic and parasympathetic nervous systems. The sympathetic system triggers the 'fight-or-flight' response, while the parasympathetic system promotes relaxation and restoration. Imbalances between these systems can occur during chronic stress, negatively impacting our health. Understanding this interplay is crucial for managing stress effectively. Practices like relaxation techniques, deep breathing, mindfulness and physical activity can activate the parasympathetic system, restore balance and enhance well-being.

Burnout is distinct from stress, as some individuals may respond positively to manageable levels of stress, finding it stimulating and motivating. However, excessive pressure and chronic stress can lead to burnout. When experiencing burnout, individuals feel emotionally depleted, mentally exhausted and devoid of motivation. Activities that were once meaningful may become challenging to engage in, and a sense of indifference or hopelessness may emerge. Burnout can leave individuals feeling empty and detached from the things that are typically important to them.

Definition: Burnout is a state of emotional, physical and mental exhaustion that arises from prolonged and excessive stress. It occurs when individuals feel overwhelmed and depleted due to the demands and pressures placed on them over an extended period.

Stress versus burnout

Stress	Burnout
Over-involvement	Lack of engagement
Intense emotions	Emotional detachment
Feeling rushed	Hopelessness
Low energy	Low motivation
Anxiety	Depression
Physical strain	Emotional exhaustion
Constant fatigue	Lack of purpose
Inability to relax	Lack of interest in activities

Stages of burnout

Signs of burnout come in many shapes and sizes and show up in many ways, and typically patterns emerge that can alert you to impending burnout. We need to recognise these warning bells before we get to a point where burnout takes over.

There are many signs of burnout and it can show up in many different ways. Place a tick next to any of the below that apply to you:

STAGE ONE

Reduced sleep quality
Unable to cope easily
Concentration and memory
  problems
Avoidance in making
  decisions
Headaches
Decreased appetite
Neglect of personal needs
  and goals
Excessive workload
Stress and mild anxiety

STAGE TWO

Cynicism
Chronic exhaustion
Resentfulness
Social withdrawal
Aggressive behaviour
Decreased sexual desire
Denial of problems
Feeling pressure
Alcohol and drug
  consumption
Lack of interest

STAGE THREE

Obsession with problems
Pessimistic outlook
Physical symptoms
Self-doubt
Social isolation
Chronic headaches
Severe neglect of personal needs
Behavioural changes
Catastrophic thoughts
Frequent illness

SEVERE BURNOUT!

Chronic sadness
Chronic mental fatigue
Chronic physical fatigue
Depression

The Art of Setting Boundaries

There are so many things you can do to prevent burnout (see page 271), but one of the most important and sizeable impacts you can make is to set boundaries.

Establishing boundaries that support you and are in alignment with your values is the first step to living the life you want, both personally and professionally. They will protect you physically, mentally and emotionally. When asked, most people agree they need boundaries but most don't have them.

Tick any of the below statements that apply to you:

- ▲ I neglect my own needs and well-being.
- ▲ I often feel guilty.
- ▲ I dislike comparing myself to others.
- ▲ I worry that prioritising myself is selfish.
- ▲ I have difficulty asserting myself and saying 'no'.
- ▲ I lack knowledge about setting healthy boundaries.
- ▲ I dislike confrontation or conflict.
- ▲ I struggle to take responsibility for my own actions.
- ▲ I feel overwhelmed and unsure of where to begin.
- ▲ I am concerned about the opinions of others.

If you have ticked any of the statements above, it could indicate that you should consider setting boundaries in your life.

The art of setting boundaries is a life-transforming habit to master daily to reinstate balance in your life. Boundaries are set to protect yourself from outside influences that rob your energy, time, health, confidence, happiness and joy. Think of boundaries as a 'no trespassing' sign that protect, nurture and nourish the asset which is you. They fuel our health and well-being, simplify life and give us space as they restore back optimal health. This 'no trespassing' sign keeps your disease to please at bay, protects your energy and keeps you connected to your true and authentic self. Boundaries ensure you are living life on purpose with self-respect and self-care.

The disease to please

People-pleasing is a behaviour driven by a strong desire to seek approval and meet others' expectations at the expense of one's own well-being. It often stems from a fear of rejection, low self-esteem or a need to avoid conflict. People-pleasers prioritise the happiness of others, sacrificing their own needs and boundaries. However, this pattern can lead to neglecting oneself, compromising values and experiencing chronic stress. Recognising the root causes of people-pleasing helps individuals establish healthier boundaries and prioritise self-care while maintaining positive relationships.

Boundaries need to be strong enough to protect you and flexible enough to allow you to grow and embrace new opportunities. They are a great indicator of your self-esteem and confidence, hence setting them is an important skill to pick up when you are feeling tired, exhausted and overwhelmed. Simple, basic, clearly defined limits for our life give us a roadmap to make decisions that support us in business and in life.

By setting effective boundaries you don't tend to take on other people's problems and stress and you are able to prioritise your own health and well-being. You learn to communicate clearly and concisely with calm confidence and often become a role model for others in the process. The result of establishing strong boundaries allows us to live the life we want to live with more energy, empathy for others, warmth, joy, clarity, vision and kindness.

Boundaries . . .

▲ Prioritise your well-being and support life in balance.

▲ Empower you to make healthy choices and take responsibility.

▲ Protect the most important person – you!

▲ Create an equal partnership.

▲ Enable you to share responsibility and power.

▲ Help you stand up for yourself and be more assertive.

▲ Build self-esteem and self-respect.

▲ Set guidelines on how you want to be treated.

The cost of not setting boundaries can result in financial burden, stress, resentment, anger, career dissatisfaction, wasted time, relationship issues and poor health. There is a negative impact in all areas of life without boundaries that can fully deplete you physically, mentally and emotionally.

Some examples of boundaries you can set include:

▲ **Time boundaries:** Setting specific times for work, rest and personal activities.

▲ **Emotional boundaries:** Recognising and honouring your own emotions without taking responsibility for others'.

▲ **Physical boundaries:** Establishing personal space and limits for your comfort and well-being.

▲ **Communication boundaries:** Expressing your needs while respecting others' and actively listening.

▲ **Relationship boundaries:** Defining acceptable behaviour and protecting your self-respect and emotions.

▲ **Financial boundaries:** Managing your finances responsibly and setting limits on giving or lending.

▲ **Personal values boundaries:** Staying true to your beliefs and not compromising for approval.

▲ **Social boundaries:** Choosing activities and connections that align with your interests and values.

▲ **Work boundaries:** Limiting workload and availability to prevent burnout and prioritise self-care.

▲ **Self-care boundaries:** Prioritising activities that nurture your well-being and not sacrificing them for others.

> Setting and maintaining boundaries empowers you to protect your energy, prioritise yourself and live a life in balance.

Five tips to clearly communicate your boundaries

1. **Be clear and direct:** Clearly express your boundaries.
2. **Set consequences:** Communicate the consequences if boundaries are crossed.
3. **Be consistent:** Reinforce your boundaries consistently.
4. **Practise active listening:** Listen actively to others' responses.
5. **Prioritise self-care:** Take care of yourself to reinforce boundaries.

Personal boundaries

Personal boundaries are essential to healthy relationships. They involve setting guidelines, rules and limits on how you want to be treated. If you don't set boundaries for yourself then someone else will set them for you and you won't like them because they won't be on your terms. Setting boundaries takes practice. It involves deciding what sort of behaviour you're happy to accept and how you'll respond if this line is crossed. Setting boundaries helps to ensure respectful relationships and to reduce conflict.

Examples of personal boundaries

▲ Setting clear limits on your time and maintaining life in balance.

▲ Defining and communicating your needs and expectations in relationships.

▲ Respecting personal space, privacy and belongings.

▲ Establishing boundaries around communication and technology use.

▲ Saying 'no' when necessary and avoiding overcommitment.

▲ Honouring your beliefs, opinions and values.

▲ Avoiding gossip and negative talk.

▲ Seeking support when needed.

Workplace boundaries

Establishing boundaries in the workplace is crucial for maintaining a healthy work environment and preserving your well-being. Workplace boundaries help define the expectations, limits and standards of behaviour you are comfortable with. Without setting boundaries, you may find yourself overwhelmed, taken advantage of or facing unnecessary stress.

Examples of workplace boundaries

▲ Defining your role and responsibilities to avoid excessive workload.

▲ Communicating your needs and expectations to colleagues and superiors.

▲ Establishing personal space and privacy.

▲ Setting boundaries on communication methods and response times.

▲ Saying 'no' when necessary and not overcommitting.

▲ Respecting your expertise and expressing your opinions.

▲ Avoiding gossip or negative talk about colleagues.

▲ Seeking support or assistance when needed.

Quick tips for setting boundaries

▲ **Define what is most important:** When it's important we make it a priority.

▲ **Set a time limit on your working day:** Establish a specific time to 'down tools', creating a clear boundary between work and personal life.

▲ **Set a technology curfew:** Set a regular time to disconnect from technology and designate tech-free zones.

▲ **Reset your focus:** Take time to refuel and restore.

▲ **Let go of guilt:** Take those guilt sandbags off your shoulders.

▲ **Take responsibility:** Your life is your responsibility, no one else's.

▲ **Know your values:** All your decision-making should be in line with your values (see Chapter 2).

▲ **Prioritise self-care:** Self-care is not selfish. It is a lifelong commitment to self (see Chapter 17 for more on this).

Take action

Reflect on what has stopped you from setting boundaries in the past.

Identify an area in your life where you need to set clear boundaries:

▲ _____

Identify three steps you can take to make others aware of your boundaries:

1. _____
2. _____
3. _____

High-Performance Burnout Prevention

Over the course of our careers, we have consistently observed high performers taking positive action to prevent burnout, using the following strategies:

Embrace self-care

Life is full of commitments, responsibilities and obligations . . . we get it. We are all leading busy lives, and it can become a struggle to fit in time for ourselves when trying to balance everything else in our lives.

One of the most common reasons many people lack self-care is because they tell themselves they don't have time – they are busy building careers, busy looking after family, busy trying to be a good friend and busy trying to keep their colleagues, employees or boss happy. We can sometimes get caught up in the 'I'm busy being busy' syndrome. Here's the thing: we should never be too busy to look after our own health and well-being and give time to what is important to us. When we tell ourselves 'I'm too busy', what we are really saying is it's not important because, when it is important, we make time for it. If building your career is important, you'll make time for it. If going to your child's concert is important, you'll make time for it. If physical activity is important, you'll make time for it. If having a strong and connected relationship with your partner is important, you'll make time for it.

Take action

▲ What's most important to you?
▲ Are you making time for it?

Practising self-care isn't always easy, but there are many things you can do to build it into your life. It's about finding the things that work best for you and then structuring them into your regular routine. This will not only improve your health and well-being but will also help you live a life that empowers you to be a fun, fulfilled, confident and vibrant human you want to share with the world.

Eight tips for elevating self-care

1. Engage in activities that bring you joy and rejuvenation.
2. Take regular breaks from technology to recharge.
3. Simplify and declutter your surroundings for mental clarity.
4. Maintain a healthy balance between giving and receiving.
5. Cultivate a gratitude practice to enhance overall well-being.
6. Pursue a passion project that ignites your creativity and fulfilment.
7. Connect with nature to find solace and serenity.
8. Intentionally schedule dedicated time for self-care activities.

Get comfortable with saying 'no'

In our interactions at work and in our daily lives, it can be difficult to utter that two-letter word: 'no'. The fear of conflict, the desire to please others and the overwhelming urge to avoid disappointing or letting people down often make it challenging to decline requests. However, when we consistently find it hard to say 'no', we may face a range of consequences. Overcommitment and overwhelm become our companions, as we neglect our personal boundaries and prioritise the needs of others over our own. The quality of our work may suffer, leading to increased stress and resentment. Moreover, our well-being takes a backseat, our energy becomes depleted and our lives can become out of balance as self-care gets sidelined amidst the constant 'yes' responses.

Below are some simple tips for confidently saying 'no' when necessary:

- ▲ **Know your priorities:** Understand your goals and commitments to assess requests confidently.
- ▲ **Be assertive:** Clearly communicate boundaries with respect.
- ▲ **Offer alternatives:** Suggest alternative solutions when you can't fulfil a request.
- ▲ **Be honest and concise:** Provide a straightforward explanation without overexplaining.
- ▲ **Stay firm and confident:** Prioritise your well-being and trust your decision.
- ▲ **Practise self-care:** Prioritise your needs and ensure you have the capacity for your responsibilities.
- ▲ **Set boundaries proactively:** Communicate availability and limitations in advance to manage expectations.
- ▲ **Practise saying 'no':** Role-play or rehearse saying 'no' to build confidence and express yourself.

Remember, confidently saying 'no' allows you to maintain balance, protect your time and energy, and focus on what matters most.

Live a life in balance

As we discussed in Chapter 9, we are not huge fans of the term 'work–life balance': we much prefer to think about it as having a 'life in balance'.

There are many ways you can create a life in balance and prioritise the things that truly matter and let go of the 'busy being busy' that takes up your time and leaves you feeling exhausted and depleted.

Today we live by an 80/20 rule for many things in our lives. This means that 80 per cent of life needs to be in balance and 20 per cent can be out of balance or a bit chaotic. The 80 per cent 'in balance' brings calmness, control, routine and happiness; however, on the flip side, we also like the chaotic 20 per cent – it makes us more resilient, strong and grateful. It teaches us how to adapt and can often help us clarify what's important.

When life isn't in 80/20 balance, it means that you are not working very smartly. As the level of chaos creeps up, we start to feel out of balance, out of control, overwhelmed and stressed. This is when it's time to take action. It's time to change something to get our lives back in balance:

▲ Eliminate non-essential tasks from your to-do list.
▲ Delegate tasks that can be handled by others.
▲ Be open to asking for help when needed.
▲ Set clear boundaries to protect your time and energy.
▲ Incorporate dedicated 'tools down' time to disconnect from technology.
▲ Consider adjusting your working hours if feasible for your well-being.

Take action

Now we want you to reflect on your life in balance:

▲ How does it look for you right now?
▲ What do you ideally want it to be?
▲ Are you prioritising what's important?

Only when you decide how you want to live your life in balance can you make changes in your life to start living that way.

Your life in balance is your responsibility. No one is going to tell you to slow down or take a load off. No one is going to make your schedule less busy for you. You must be good to yourself before you can be good to others.

Shannah: Most people feel stages of burnout at all the different ages and stages of life. I loved working in my twenties and had the most amazing, fun, high-octane job, filled with sport, travel, dinners and networking with elite performers. But that was on weekends as the sport events I worked on were not held during the week. So I would work all week on the paperwork, meetings and planning side of things and then go to sport events over the weekend. My mind wanted to keep going but my body was not happy. I pushed headaches, lethargy, insomnia and personal recovery aside and kept telling myself to harden up. One day I just couldn't get up; I literally could not lift my head off the pillow. This was the beginning of a very rapid decline as my body was telling me 'enough is enough; if you won't listen to the signals, I will shut you down'.

Chronic fatigue syndrome robbed me of the ability to go for a walk, work, socialise, do housework – total shutdown. An overwhelming tiredness like I had never experienced before, extreme mental and physical exhaustion, muscle pain, joint pain, unrefreshing sleep, unable to think clearly or remember much, I was thrust into the hurt locker. It was horrific. This was in 2000 when no one had really heard of it, there was no research on it, so all doctors were stumped. It took years for me to get moving again and over the past twenty years my health and boundaries have been front and centre, protecting the asset which is myself. I will never allow myself to abuse my mind and body like that again.

Life in balance is a game changer!

'Embrace the pace' has been my motto and what I call 'sprinting', for me, can only be done a few days at a time for big projects with recovery built in. I have built in boundaries in my life, work with a naturopath to boost my adrenals, have regular acupuncture and massage, and protect my sleep as much as I can to ensure I feel great energy in my quest for longevity and vitality in life.

Burnout summary

1. Burnout is a state of complete physical, mental and emotional exhaustion.
2. Too much stress can lead to burnout. But stress and burnout are not the same.
3. Burnout happens when we don't make ourselves the asset and set boundaries.
4. Boundaries are 'no trespassing' signs that protect, nurture and nourish our physical, mental and emotional health.
5. Nurturing a life in balance is your personal journey.

Create Your Personal High-Performance Plan: BURNOUT

Do you recognise any of the symptoms on page 264? If so, what stage of burnout are you in?

_____

_____

To prevent burnout:

What do you need to STOP doing?

1. _____

_____

2. _____

_____

3. _____

_____

What do you need to START doing?

1. _____

_____

2. _____

_____

3. _____

_____

What do you need to KEEP doing?

1. _____

_____

2. _____

_____

3. _____

_____

Chapter 14

Master High-Performance Planning

It takes as much energy to wish as it does to plan

ELEANOR ROOSEVELT

You now know your values, your vision, your goals, the habits you want to implement and the type of leader you want to be in life, for yourself and others. Now is the time to plan like a pro so you not only achieve success, but protect your time, space, energy and health at the same time.

A plan is a course of action, a central map that provides focus and outlines how you will get to your big, bold vision. A plan states in advance how the work is to be done and provides direction for action and, most importantly, a timeframe. An action plan gives the brain the map it craves.

It is incredible when we speak and ask an audience, 'Who here has a cracking written plan that excites you?' Most often, only 20 per cent firmly raise their hand, owning it, loving it and you can see they have really done the work and are seasoned planners and action-orientated people.

Many people want everything all at once – the career, the family, the fun, the friends, the health, the time out – and in order to embrace a sustainable pace and find success in all areas, we need to see it all on a plan.

To master your life, to manage yourself for high performance, you need the power skill of planning and time management so you can take serious action. It is the process of organising, deciding and fine-tuning your time and, when you get it right, you will end up working smarter not harder. High achievers, who thrive in their goals without burnout, are exceptional creators of plans and military managers of their time.

Planning takes time, but we promise it is time well spent!

Everything you put into your plan and diary is a choice – your choice. If you don't plan your life, someone else will.

The Benefits of Planning

A powerful strategic plan and exceptional time-management skills will allow you to live with confidence, clarity of direction and a heightened sense of well-being. Productive world-class planning amplifies and heightens your success in life, supports your long-term sustainability and integrates your goals from all parts of your life.

Helps reduce stress

Planning helps you reduce the uncertainties of your future as it involves anticipation of future events. Stress decreases when you know where you are going and when. If you want to run a marathon, there is a training and race plan so you are paced and can finish strong. Goals such as paying off a mortgage need a plan over a decade, then a year, then a month for action to be taken.

Fires up motivation and commitment

When you get lost in the day-to-day of 'doing' and focusing on tasks, you can lose sight of where you are going. The plan, the map, is there to support the dream. Olympians need to complete the daily training and recovery but be reminded of the plan that they are working towards on the journey to qualify for Olympic selection. Looking at your plan you know what comes next and you can see where you came from.

Allows for flexibility

When you have a plan you will no doubt encounter some 'detours' as there is nothing more certain in this life than change. You can be prepared for Plan B, the pivot or when circumstances change, and slightly alter the vision, goal and plan.

High-Performance Planning for Elevated Results

Have you ever wondered how elite athletes maintain focus, discipline and energy between four-year Olympic cycles and juggle this with family obligations, serious recovery and maintaining important friendships? Similar to ultra-productive people, they are dedicated to scheduling everything on calendars and have a clear plan and priorities.

Planning is creating your main map supporting your values, vision, goals, tasks and habits, and scheduling it, breaking it down, so action can be taken. It is like planning a road trip: you choose your destination and plan the trip so you feel excited, you visualise it, you feel it and you are in the driver's seat, both hands on the wheel. With the directions put in the GPS, you are ready to enjoy the journey knowing where you need to stop and fuel and where you need to arrive each night in order to end up at the grand destination.

Many people know their vision and have some goals and habits for the year, but lack a well-thought-through plan. This is when strategic planning comes into play, taking everything up a step and going into a little more detail than perhaps you are used to. The plan is laid out to show you the pathway to achieving your goals with less stress, anxiety, overwhelm and exhaustion.

Plan in years
Fine-tune in seasons
Work in months
Live in days

Choose the right planner for you

We all have different personalities, preferences, responsibilities, roles and time schedules, so it's important to choose the planner that works best for you. Some people prefer technology, using apps; others prefer paper and pen. At the end of the day, your mind needs to visually see the map in front of you to know where you are going, to know what comes next and to reflect and see what has been done, hence the saying, 'If you don't record it, you don't own it.'

Consider purchasing the following three items to support you in effective planning:

1. A wall planner.
2. A week-to-page diary.
3. A to-do list.

Seasonal planning

The first step in high-performance planning is creating an annual plan – getting a bird's eye view of the year ahead.

Start with a piece of paper. Divide it into either quarters or seasons. Plot the following on to each quarter:

We have twelve months, 365 days to play with each year. Do you want to elevate and plot some markers down that will guide you to success?

- ▲ Birthdays/anniversaries.
- ▲ Public/school holidays.
- ▲ Annual work commitments, such as conferences, trade shows, buying trips.
- ▲ Main goals for each season: what you want to learn each season.

▲ What habit you want to master in each thirteen-week block.

▲ Your holidays (time out).

▲ Personal courses booked, retreats, books you want to read.

▲ Annual medical and dental check-ups.

▲ Annual tax time.

▲ Personal non-negotiables: gym, massage, facials, blood work, naturopath, etc.

Planning around the seasons is a great way to harness your time and set your tone for the year ahead. The seasons have their own individual energies, and that energy can be tapped into as you plan out your year.

Planning in seasons is one of the easiest planning methods to implement. As weather changes in each season, you can tap into how you want to feel in each season, how you dress differently, eat differently and exercise differently, and associate yearly must-dos with certain times of the year. There is rhythm and ritual in seasons that nature displays, and you too can flow with the seasons. Taxes are due in winter, outdoor events and barbeques are in summer, decluttering happens in spring. Seasonal planning is about planning the way you live and work with the already established regular seasonal events.

Treat the four quadrants like a chess board, moving pieces until the four areas sing to you, feel right and are structured for you to enjoy the seasons and how you feel in them: what activities and habits support you best in each, which seasons' goals will be set and which seasons' goals will be completed.

Life is a series of seasons. Creativity is a series of seasons. Productivity is a series of seasons. Elite performance is a series of seasons.

Spring: offers you the gift of new energy, fresh and vibrant. You could consider this time to be an opportunity to 'spring clean' any projects you may have on the go, releasing any old energy and inviting in the new. It is a great time to do your annual medical check-up, dentist appointment, car service, prune shrubs after they bloom and fully declutter the house.

Summer: hosted by the sun, you are invited to shine brightly in these months, to be present in the world around you, exploring, adventuring, bathing in the glorious sunlight. It is a time to refuel and embrace life with reinvigorated energy and joy. It is a great time to do outdoor projects, fire up your fun, get creative and learn something new.

Autumn: brings you the energy of transition. It is a glorious time of dancing light and changing colours with energy to create change as the heat leaves us. When considering the energy of autumn within your planning, consider it a time to start something big after the fun of summer, to start a project which can set you up for your best year yet. It is a great time to really delve into those bigger goals.

Winter: traditionally, winter is a time of reflection, hibernation and contemplation. You nestle into the indoor warmth that surrounds you, you quiet the mind and still the soul as social arrangements quieten. In modern times, winter may be the time when you work the hardest. It's cold outside, and those summer activities are not around to distract you, so you could be at your most productive. However, bear in mind that, without a cycle or season of recovery, burnout and depletion occur. High performance without refuel-ling and pausing leads to depletion. Consider your habits and behaviours in the winter months and how you can harness the energy to work for you. It is a great time to complete your tax, feed the garden at the end of winter and put some laser focus, effort and time into your big goals.

Take action

▲ What season is your favourite?
▲ How do you feel in each season?
▲ In what season do you set the most goals?
▲ In what season do you want to have the most time off?
▲ What actions can you take in each season?

Once every three months (generally every thirteen weeks), plan, set goals and celebrate your achievements. These planning sessions should also include time for reflection and for the reviewing of finished and in-progress tasks.

MY SPRING PLAN

MY STRENGTHS	MY VALUES	BOOKS TO READ/PODCASTS

I AM THE ASSET

MY BOOKENDS AM	HABITS TO IMBED	MY MOVEMENT PLAN
MY BOOKENDS PM	MY WORK GOALS	MY PERSONAL GOALS

REGULAR SPRING APPOINTMENTS		MY FUN LIST
MY AFFIRMATION	MY NUTRITION PLAN	

MY SUMMER PLAN

MY STRENGTHS	MY VALUES	BOOKS TO READ/PODCASTS

I AM THE ASSET

MY BOOKENDS AM	HABITS TO IMBED	MY MOVEMENT PLAN
MY BOOKENDS PM	MY WORK GOALS	MY PERSONAL GOALS
REGULAR SUMMER APPOINTMENTS		MY FUN LIST
MY AFFIRMATION	MY NUTRITION PLAN	

MY AUTUMN PLAN

MY STRENGTHS	MY VALUES	BOOKS TO READ/PODCASTS

I AM THE ASSET

MY BOOKENDS AM	HABITS TO IMBED	MY MOVEMENT PLAN
MY BOOKENDS PM	MY WORK GOALS	MY PERSONAL GOALS

REGULAR AUTUMN APPOINTMENTS		MY FUN LIST
MY AFFIRMATION	MY NUTRITION PLAN	

MY WINTER PLAN

MY STRENGTHS	MY VALUES	BOOKS TO READ/PODCASTS

I AM THE ASSET

MY BOOKENDS AM	HABITS TO IMBED	MY MOVEMENT PLAN
MY BOOKENDS PM	MY WORK GOALS	MY PERSONAL GOALS

REGULAR WINTER APPOINTMENTS		MY FUN LIST
MY AFFIRMATION	MY NUTRITION PLAN	

Australian ex-Olympian Toby Jenkins also has this great advice: 'Find someone whose work you trust and admire who has already done specifically what you want to do. Ask them for help, what their plan was, and then filter their advice for your own situation. It's not about saving an hour here or there. It's about saving you potentially years to get to your goal.'

Monthly planning

From yearly planning you can then go into monthly planning where you break out goals from the yearly plan and shape them into something more tactical.

What gets scheduled gets done.

Monthly planning involves using a monthly planner/diary to organise the next four-week block of time. It is like an overview or summary of all your important goals for the month. Starting with a monthly spread where you can visibly see four weeks is key. Use it for budgeting, work projects, savings, major regular appointments, deadlines and main family commitments, birthdays or home projects.

Take action

▲ Schedule in your monthly commitments for your work and projects.

▲ Schedule in kids' arrangements, sports, school and social commitments.

▲ Schedule in time out – book your own space, your meeting with self, your free time.

▲ Schedule in some fun – date nights, catch-ups with friends, hobby time, food preparation time, exercise and planning time.

Does the month excite you or does it look over-scheduled? Do you need to cut back on something? Say no to something? Cancel something? Are you being your own time-robber by putting in too many things? Have you put in recovery time? Remember it is OK to say the gracious 'no' (see page 273).

Weekly planning

You now have a base to define your day-to-day activities, create habits and allocate time to get you to those goals in your weekly – and then daily – plan. The premise of this is that you can use all of the information you have gathered in the preceding pages to take those big goals that can seem daunting and chunk them down to what you need to do on any particular day.

Weekly planning is about organising your daily plans while seeing the entire week at a glance including your weekly habits. Get into the habit of planning two weeks ahead, time-blocking for projects to be completed, self-care, friends, family and recovery. Visually seeing your week mapped out prepares the mind and allows you to pace your energy and move things that you see won't work for you.

Sunday night is traditionally when you prime the brain for the week ahead. A clear outline of the week ahead allows you to prepare the mind, the energy and the emotions. Look at the week, ponder, refine and recreate the week for the best results focusing in on controlling what you can control. Ask yourself – does this work for me? Do I feel in control? What mindset do I need? How do I want to show up?

Control the controllable

As humans we often spend so much valuable time trying to control the things that are out of our control and, when we do this, we end up frustrated, angry and depleted of our energy. Change the narrative and focus on only controlling the controllable. If you start getting annoyed at yourself or a situation, are not happy with how things are going or are not getting the result you want, ask yourself: is this something that's in my control? If the answer is no, quickly move on and don't waste time or energy on something that is going to make you unhappy. Your focus can instead turn to thinking about what you can control and what's going to bring you happiness today.

Daily planning

The focus of your day can now be fine-tuning your habits around the tasks that need to be completed. The golden rule is to plan your day in advance, the night before. A daily plan shows the details of the hours and the key here is consistency and visibility. It only takes around two minutes to write a quick list of everything that is essential for you to do the following day – appointment times, what time you will exercise, meal prep, attend a meeting, catch up with a friend. It is liberating to feel organised and ready.

Be flexible

When you are planning and writing these wonderful seasonal, monthly, weekly and daily roadmaps to support your mind and your precious energy, nothing is totally set in stone. Your plans need to be malleable. Know that life gets in the way sometimes: you may get sick, or have a sick child or parent, or have an accident, or things may not go perfectly to plan, so allowing some flexibility, some adaptability, makes for a smoother ride.

How to Take Action

Are you one to overcommit, over-schedule and over-do, all at the expense of your own health, well-being, happiness and confidence? Our clients often talk about their time as if there were a time famine, but this is a result of a lack of clear and strategic planning. Once you have a plan, you need to manage your time so you can take massive action.

Create a to-do list

These are your tiny tasks, the small things to do in between the set meetings and appointments. There are three types of to-do list to choose from: a handwritten list which you then tick off when a task is completed; a bullet-pointed journal; or to-do list apps which are most popular today. Prioritise your small tasks in order of urgency and importance. To avoid procrastination, do the hardest thing first.

The expression 'eat that frog' refers to the idea of tackling your most challenging or unpleasant task first thing in the morning, instead of procrastinating or avoiding it. By addressing the most difficult task right away, you can gain a sense of accomplishment, reduce stress and increase overall productivity throughout the day.

To excite yourself and elevate your energy, call your 'to-do' list your 'joy list'; your 'I get-to-do' list rather than your 'I have-to-do' list. It will change your energy instantly. You *get* to write that proposal or that book; you don't *have* to. You *get* to wash your family's clothes, pick up the kids from school, have dinner with your family or friends, see your parents, go to the gym; you don't *have* to. Reframing your to-do list in this way is a powerful tool to change up your energy.

To effectively manage your tasks and enhance your productivity, follow these simple steps:

1. **Identify your tiny tasks:** Take note of the small things that need to be done, between your meetings and appointments.
2. **Prioritise based on urgency and importance:** Begin each day by identifying your five MITs (Most Important Things) and prioritise their completion. Focus on these key tasks first, and success will follow.
3. **Tick off completed tasks:** As you complete each task, mark it as done on your list.
4. **Stay focused and disciplined:** Maintain your focus throughout the day and stick to the tasks outlined on your to-do list, resisting the temptation to get side-tracked.

5. **Review and update regularly:** Take time to review and update your to-do list regularly, adding new tasks and adjusting priorities as needed.

Review, acknowledge and celebrate

Confidence, motivation and inspiration need fuel. You need to see progress. When you don't pat yourself on the back, acknowledge your effort or tick off things, it is hard to keep going, to stay on track and stay inspired. When you tick off things, high-five someone when a task is complete, give a gold star, ring the bell or whatever it is for you, you fuel your sense of achievement, feel good about yourself, boost your own confidence and upgrade your energy. You are making progress. You feel great.

Celebrating your small successes is a critical step so many forget to take.

In a world filled with endless opportunities and demands, one of the greatest time-wasters is attempting to do it all.

Take action

▲ What can you celebrate about yourself today?
▲ What did you achieve today?
▲ How did you show up today?

Look in the mirror and be proud.

High-performance planning to this level is stepping up and is essential for anyone who desires longevity of motivation and inspiration, and avoiding burnout. It is the ultimate self-management tool to pace yourself and your year. It is like taking that road trip: when you have planned how to get there, know roughly how far you've got to go and how long it will take, you have a far better chance of enjoying the drive. Review and celebration is stopping to take the photo, feeling where you are in the moment and appreciating the road just travelled before you get back in and head to the next town.

Managing your time will take your performance to the next level, both personally and professionally, and allow you to perform your tasks and develop your habits with purpose and intent. It doesn't matter if you are a CEO, a business owner, a parent, a student or a child, planning is essential to upgrading your life.

Colleen: When it comes to planning there are several things I can't live without, and my calendar is one of them. Call me old-fashioned, but I still have a handwritten calendar – there's something about committing pen to paper, rather than using a digital calendar, that works for me. Everything goes in it: work meetings, family events, social activities, catch-ups with friends, personal appointments, date nights, me time and exercise. I even write in my calendar to walk every day. It is a way I hold myself accountable.

Not only do I write everything in my calendar, but I also colour-code it. Every different area of my life is denoted by a different coloured highlighter. I do this so I have a quick reference to not only what's in for the month but I can also easily see if one colour is standing out more than another. When I see too much purple being highlighted, for example, it means that I am over-committing to work and business engagements, and need to have a rethink to get a little more balance in my life.

Putting pen to paper will help you to prioritise, and the result is a great feeling of confidence and freedom. Remind yourself before you start that clarity is key and know what is essential for you to feel confident, know your non-negotiables for your health and your family and where your boundaries lie.

What is your grand plan?	(the destination)	(your grand vision)
What is your monthly plan?	(the main towns)	(your set goals)
What is your weekly plan?	(the small towns)	(your main tasks)
What is your daily plan?	(the daily drive)	(your power habits)

Planning summary

1. Create your year in seasons/quarters with the big-ticket items.
2. Plan your month with great actions and space to rest and review.
3. Design your week with clarity and prioritisation.
4. Own your day and write your 'get-to-do' list the night before.
5. Put pen to paper to really understand your time: feel it, own it.

Create Your Personal High-Performance Plan: PLANNING

To elevate your plan:

What do you need to STOP doing?

1. _____
_____

2. _____
_____

3. _____
_____

What do you need to START doing?

1. _____
_____

2. _____
_____

3. _____
_____

What do you need to KEEP doing?

1. _____
_____

2. _____
_____

3. _____
_____

Chapter 15

Find Your Happiness

Happiness depends upon ourselves

ARISTOTLE

t's now time to elevate your happiness! While happiness can be defined in many different ways, it is often described as a state of emotional well-being characterised by feelings of contentment, joy and fulfilment. It comes and goes and, unfortunately, for many it is often viewed in terms of using other people as a benchmark. Though comparisonitis and judgement can be used to motivate you to lift to greater heights, for the majority they are the thief of joy and happiness.

Happiness is achieved by having a purpose, feeling healthy and having a sense of meaning in life. It is an inside job in that it comes from within.

Happiness is . . .

▲ A conscious choice we make.
▲ A habit we develop through positive actions.
▲ Embracing our imperfections and accepting ourselves fully.
▲ Living a life that aligns with our choices and values.
▲ Cultivating an optimistic outlook on life.
▲ Appreciating and expressing gratitude for what we have.
▲ Nurturing a deep love and acceptance for ourselves.
▲ Feeling a sense of contentment and fulfilment.

The Science of Happiness

In the late eighties, psychologist Mihaly Csikszentmihalyi carried out a scientific study of 'what makes happy people happy' and provided a simple framework for us to elevate and upgrade our experience of happiness: 50 | 40 | 10:

Our genes affect 50 per cent of our happiness: Half of our happiness depends on the genes we inherit. The unique genes passed down from our parents shape our general level of happiness. Some people luck out with a cheerful disposition, naturally focusing on life's positives, while others tend towards negativity. Scientists often refer to this as a 'happiness set point'.

External factors affect 10 per cent of our happiness: A mere 10 per cent of our happiness is influenced by external conditions. Things such as our career, our relationships, our location, the climate, our finances, our health, our physical appearance and our material possessions collectively account for just a fraction of our ongoing happiness.

Our choices and thoughts affect 40 per cent of our happiness: A significant 40 per cent of our happiness is shaped by what we do and how we think. This means you have control over almost half of your happiness:

1. Engage in activities that bring you joy and satisfaction, whether that be pursuing hobbies, indulging in your favourite pastimes or simply taking time to relax and unwind.
2. Seek out experiences that elicit positive emotions and bring a sense of pleasure, such as spending time with loved ones, enjoying nature, listening to music or savouring delicious food.
3. Prioritise self-care and activities that promote your physical and mental well-being, as taking care of yourself can contribute to a greater sense of pleasure and overall happiness.

Many studies have shown that these activities sustainably increase happiness in the long term.

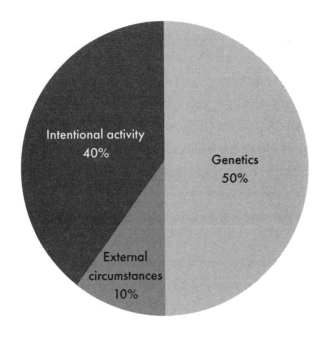

Intentional activity
40%

Genetics
50%

External
circumstances
10%

**Change IS
possible.**
We can sustainably
increase our own
happiness and
many of these
habits and activities
take just a few
minutes a day.

Five High-Performance Happiness Skills

The purpose of life is to be happy.
— the Dalai Lama

Gratitude	**Kindness**	**Empathy**	**Journaling**	**Affirmations**
Write down three things you are grateful for every day	Practise random acts of kindness	Put yourself in other people's shoes	Write your thoughts and feelings to create clarity	Manifest through positive statement training

Gratitude

As we explored on page 115, gratitude is an emotional state and a fundamental attitude needed to embrace and live a great life peppered with happiness, joy and a feeling of fulfilment. People who adopt gratitude as a way of living by regularly reflecting on things they are grateful for experience and express more positive emotions, sleep better and experience other health-related benefits.

A heart filled with gratitude attracts miracles.

Instead of becoming preoccupied with the future or worrying about the past, focus your attention on the present moment and all its richness.

There has been plenty of research around gratitude showing that it is the easiest and quickest way to fill your happiness tank. Scientists have found that people who practise gratitude consistently experience a host of benefits such as:

▲ Lower blood pressure and improved immune function.
▲ More positive emotions, such as happiness and optimism.
▲ Expressing greater compassion, kindness and generosity.
▲ Stronger relationships and decreased loneliness.

These are fairly compelling reasons to have gratitude as a part of your daily routine. Building in a gratitude habit stands you in good stead for hardwiring happiness and feeling more joy.

In life the object of gratitude can vary:

▲ It might be directed towards other people, such as family, friends, colleagues, mentors or leaders.

▲ It might be directed towards living and non-living objects.

▲ It might be directed towards experiences, opportunities and events.

The most powerful way to dip into the skill and habit of gratitude is to start noticing what is around you and acknowledging it. The second is to write it down. As you'll have discovered throughout this book, seeing the written word is far more powerful than just thinking it.

Start a gratitude journal and begin with three things you are grateful for each day. Watch the list grow and your experience of daily happiness change.

Thought-starters

Relaxing weekends.	Memorable road trips.
Invigorating hot showers.	Wisdom shared by grandparents.
Soul-stirring music.	Growth through challenges.
Vibrant colours that inspire.	Comfortable shoes for every step.
Fulfilling career pursuits.	Treasured photographs and memories.

Take action

Try it now: What are you most grateful for today?

1. _____

2. _____

3. _____

30 days of gratitude

1. What is the moment you were most grateful for today?	**2.** Which place are you most grateful for?	**3.** What physical attribute are you most grateful for?
4. What talent do you possess that you are grateful for?	**5.** What is the title of the book you are most grateful for?	**6.** What is the memory you are most grateful for?
7. Who is the childhood friend you are most grateful for?	**8.** What is the opportunity you're most grateful for?	**9.** What personality trait do you possess that you are grateful for?
10. What is the film that has brought you the most happiness?	**11.** What is the music you are most grateful for at the moment?	**12.** What aspect of your childhood are you most grateful for today?
13. What has happened this year that you are grateful for?	**14.** What success have you been grateful for most recently?	**15.** What did you hear today that you are grateful for?

16. Which family member are you most grateful for today?	**17.** What did you do today that made you happy?	**18.** What past challenge do you feel thankful for today?
19. Which colleagues or mentors do you feel particularly grateful to?	**20.** What moment this week are you particularly grateful for?	**21.** What knowledge do you feel thankful for most often?
22. What sight made you feel grateful today?	**23.** Which friend do you feel most thankful for today?	**24.** What act of kindness are you grateful for today?
25. What happened today that you feel thankful for?	**26.** What aspect of the place you live in makes you most grateful?	**27.** What new experience have you been grateful for lately?
28. What new thing did you learn today?	**29.** What colour did you see today that you are grateful for?	**30.** What has happened this month that you are grateful for?

Kindness

Kindness and random acts of compassion towards others (see page 86) are a major key to becoming happier. Both spontaneous and planned acts of kindness, such as helping someone cross the road or volunteering, add to our happiness and well-being.

In a world where we can be anything, be kind.

Thought-starters

Pay it forward and buy the next coffee.	Send a postcard to a loved one.
Donate clothes and toys to charity.	Bake something for your neighbour.
Write positive thanks on someone's blog.	Create a care package for someone in need.
Offer a friend a lift.	Donate blood.
Give up your seat on public transport.	Pick up litter at your park.

Take action

Think about what random acts of kindness you want to build into your days:

1. _____
2. _____
3. _____

Empathy

Empathy is the ability to sense other people's emotions, coupled with being able to imagine what someone else might be thinking or feeling. It is the skill of emotionally understanding what other people feel, seeing things from their point of view and imagining yourself in their place. This helps you maintain stronger and more successful relationships in both personal and professional contexts. The golden rule – 'Treat others as you would like to be treated yourself' – is the foundational piece to start your practice from.

Shine brightly as a beacon of compassion, kindness and inspiration, guiding others towards their own inner light.

Three types of empathy

Affective empathy: The ability to respond appropriately to other people's emotions.

Somatic empathy: The ability to physically experience what another person is feeling.

Cognitive empathy: The ability to understand someone's response and what they might be thinking.

Thought-starters

Listen without interruption.

Try to understand people even when you don't agree with them.

Pay attention to body language and other types of non-verbal communication.

Imagine yourself in another person's shoes.

Be willing and vulnerable to express how you are feeling.

Park your own judgement.

Take action

How will you elevate your empathy towards others?

1. _____

2. _____

3. _____

Journaling

A journal is a written record of your experiences, thoughts and observations. Journaling allows you to process thoughts at a deeper level. Doing this daily will elevate and upgrade your life.

Maintaining a daily journal is one of the best initiatives you will ever take to deepen your happiness, clarify your thoughts, record your daily acts of

Journaling takes us on a transformative voyage, navigating the depths of our inner world, unlocking self-discovery and guiding us towards profound growth.

progress, record your wins and unlock your thinking. You will develop self-awareness, clarify intentions and remain focused on the things that truly count. Research has revealed that regularly keeping a journal improves mental focus and self-confidence as your self-awareness is sharpened.

There is no right or wrong way to journal, but you can get a notebook and a pen and just get started, either writing morning or night:

1. Record daily acts of progress.
2. Record daily insights.
3. Record your gratitude.
4. Release your worries.

Thought-starters

Write your daily insights and learnings.

Write things you want to learn and try.

Write what makes you happy.

Write down what you need to let go of.

Write about your perfect day.

Write about a memory.

Write about a problem you have solved.

Write about a fear you have and how you will overcome it.

Write reasons to be proud of yourself.

Write quotes you found that day.

Take action

What main topics do you want to journal about?

1. _____
2. _____
3. _____

Affirmations

Your mindset and your words are a fundamental part of happiness and success. The
word 'affirmation' comes from the Latin
affirmare, which means to 'make steady,
strengthen'. Positive affirmation helps break
patterns of negative thoughts and move you
towards more positive feelings and actions.

> A single word or sentence has the power to change your thoughts.

Affirmations are a wonderful tool to use to replace any negative
self-talk that may be running consistently in your mind. While
they may feel 'untrue' initially, when recited consistently and
consciously, affirmations are the first step to forming new beliefs
and neural pathways.

Thought-starters

- ▲ 'I choose happiness and wellness.'
- ▲ 'I am open to abundance.'
- ▲ 'Today is a gift I embrace with positivity.'
- ▲ 'I am unique.'
- ▲ 'I am strong.'
- ▲ 'I forgive those who have harmed me and peacefully
  detach from them.'

- ▲ 'I know great things are happening.'
- ▲ 'Everything happening now is for me, not to me.'
- ▲ 'I choose to feel free.'
- ▲ 'I am improving every day.'

Take action

What would you like to start believing about yourself? What would you like to be true? To love yourself deeply and bravely? To invite in love, joy and vitality every day?

What are your three power affirmations for happiness?

1. _____
2. _____
3. _____

Strong social relationships are the most important contributor to enduring happiness for most people, so nurture yourself, nurture your relationships, friends and family, and elevate happiness around the world, one moment, one smile, one conversation at a time.

It is time for you to get into your happy!

Shannah: Happiness is something I have cultivated over time as I don't wake up happy naturally. As a child I thought I was a glass-half-full human; however, as I have aged, I have come to the realisation that I am possibly glass-half-empty genetically, so focusing on the 40 per cent that is truly in my control each day has been a focus over the past decade.

I have loved journaling, unlocking my thoughts, drawing, collecting words, quotes and recording the day, my thoughts, feelings and dreams. I have suffered from some debilitating depression in the past so creating habits that boost my feelings of happiness, gratitude and joy have been a focus as they are in my control.

Having affirmations on the wall or written on the mirror in whiteboard marker has felt like the biggest support system for my mind and emotions. Seeing them daily, they have now become a part of me. Saying to myself, 'I love myself, I love my full [rather than busy] life' has given me incredible joy and confidence along with living a life of gratitude and noticing the smallest of things.

Happiness summary

1. Happiness is mostly an inside job.
2. Forty per cent of our happiness comes from intentional activities – both thoughts and behaviour.
3. Gratitude, kindness, empathy, journaling and affirmations are skills to work on for a happier life.
4. Happiness is a habit.
5. Humans crave pleasure, engagement and meaning.

Look at the list below:

▲ Explore somewhere new.
▲ Have a picnic.
▲ Visit a museum.
▲ Sit by a river and sketch.
▲ Go to a musical or the theatre.
▲ Get up early and watch the sunrise.
▲ Go for a swim.

▲ Cook something new.

▲ Ride your bike to work.

▲ Give a compliment.

▲ Organise a date night with your partner or a catch-up with friends.

▲ Try learning a new language or a musical instrument.

▲ Go camping.

▲ Meditate.

What inspires you? What lifts you and fills your happiness tank?

_____

_____

_____

_____

The more of these nourishing activities we do, the more we believe in ourselves. Make the time – guilt-free – as these activities will bring out the best in you, enabling you to flourish and shine for those you care about most.

Create Your Personal High-Performance Plan: HAPPINESS

To elevate your happiness:

What do you need to STOP doing?

1. _____
   _____
2. _____
   _____
3. _____

What do you need to START doing?

1. _____
   _____
2. _____
   _____
3. _____
   _____

What do you need to KEEP doing?

1. _____
   _____
2. _____
   _____
3. _____
   _____

Chapter 16

Live a Deeply Fulfilled Life

Deep human connection
is . . . the purpose and
the result of a meaningful
life – and it will inspire the
most amazing acts of love,
generosity and humanity

MELINDA GATES

Many of us focus on achievement as a marker of living a fulfilled life, as it has been that way since primary school – get the grades, make the team, make the friends, and so on. So why are so many of us still not fulfilled? We are taught to expect to be happy when we achieve our goals – pay off the mortgage, buy the car, lose the weight, reach a personal best, get the promotion, find the partner – and yet for many it is not enough; there is something missing.

Many people are incredibly successful, but feel empty and hollow inside, as achievement has a tendency to be very addictive. That is why for many it is hard to walk away from their sport, their profession or their career even when, in reality, it is all over. Your achievements become your identity, your focus, your source of joy. When your passion for the game or your job wanes, you stay as your sport or job is no longer what you do, but who you are.

Take action

Think about:

- ▲ Who are you without the hats you wear?
- ▲ Who are you without the job you do?
- ▲ Who are you without the accolades?
- ▲ Who are you without the career title?

Michael Phelps, world-class Olympic swimmer, has shared that his success came at a price. After his retirement following the London 2012 Summer Olympics, Phelps checked himself into rehab. 'I thought of myself as a swimmer, and nothing else,' he said in an interview.

After a break, with a new perspective and feeling of purpose, Phelps came out of retirement and attended the Rio 2016 Summer Olympics. He won gold, ending his career with a sense of accomplishment and satisfaction. He planned his life outside sport – new chapters for ages and stages of his life.

Having your identity tied up solely with what you do for a living can turn toxic. Achievement without fulfilment is an empty place. When you take the time to turn expectations into appreciation, you achieve greater clarity and alter your definition of success.

The journey towards a more fulfilling existence starts within you. Fulfilment is living a life of purpose and satisfaction. It is feeling deep meaning, experiencing joy in your vision and your dreams, and living in full alignment and flow with your values.

Different from happiness, fulfilment is about embracing a whole range of emotions and is the process of living a valued life where you pursue things that matter to you or that you are passionate about.

> Fulfilment is always tied to a sense of purpose.

Fulfilment comes from knowing who you are, what you want, who you want to become, how you want to feel in the process and the purpose of it all. It is a feeling of peace, that you know there is purpose to your actions and they are connected to your values, beliefs and morals.

Fulfilment in life increases as you age, as with each year you live you gain more knowledge, life experience and expertise that can be shared. It is a long-lasting, internal sense of wholeness, in which we find value in recognising our personal impact on the world around us.

What Does Success Mean to You?

Success is a deeply personal concept that varies from person to person. It goes beyond external achievements and material possessions, reflecting individual values, aspirations and fulfilment. For some, success may be finding purpose and meaning in their work, while for others, it could be nurturing meaningful relationships or making a positive impact on their community. Success might mean personal growth, overcoming challenges or achieving a desired life in balance. It could be embracing one's unique talents and passions, living authentically or finding inner peace and happiness. Ultimately, success is defined by you and the goals that resonate with your heart and soul.

Take action

Take a moment to reflect on what success means to you. Consider the specific examples in the table below that align with your own vision of a fulfilling and meaningful life.

	Career Success Metrics	Personal Success Metrics
Objective	▲ Annual salary or income growth: Achieving a 10 per cent increase in annual salary or income compared to the previous year. ▲ Number of promotions or advancements: Securing two promotions within a five-year timeframe. ▲ Client or customer satisfaction ratings: Maintaining a client satisfaction rating of 90 per cent or above based on regular surveys. ▲ Project completion rate: Successfully completing 95 per cent of assigned projects within the specified timeframe. ▲ Sales or revenue targets achieved: Meeting or exceeding quarterly sales targets by 15 per cent.	▲ Health and fitness metrics: Achieving a target body mass index of 25 or lower through regular exercise and healthy eating. ▲ Financial stability: Saving 20 per cent of monthly income and reducing overall debt by 15 per cent over a one-year period. ▲ Educational or skill development achievements: Completing a professional certification or acquiring a new skill relevant to career growth. ▲ Philanthropic or volunteer contributions: Volunteering for one hundred hours a year at a local community organisation or contributing to a charity of choice. ▲ Personal projects or goals completed: Successfully finishing a personal project, such as writing a book or completing a marathon.

Subjective

Career Success Metrics	Personal Success Metrics
▲ Job satisfaction or fulfilment: Reporting a consistent high level of job satisfaction and fulfilment during performance evaluations.	▲ Happiness and well-being: Maintaining a consistent sense of happiness and overall well-being in daily life.
▲ Life in balance: Maintaining a healthy balance and dedicating quality time to professional networking.	▲ Strong relationships and social connections: Cultivating and nurturing meaningful relationships with family, friends and colleagues.
▲ Recognition or awards received: Receiving two company-wide recognition awards for exceptional performance and contributions.	▲ Work–life integration: Balancing professional commitments with personal interests and responsibilities.
▲ Positive feedback from colleagues or superiors: Consistently receiving positive feedback and recognition from colleagues and superiors.	▲ Emotional intelligence and self-awareness: Demonstrating self-awareness and emotional intelligence in personal interactions and decision-making.
▲ Personal growth and development opportunities: Actively participating in at least three professional development programs or courses per year.	▲ Overall life satisfaction: Feeling content and satisfied with life as a whole, including personal achievements and relationships.

How to Experience Fulfilment

Visualise success

Visualise your future goals coming to life and challenge yourself to grow.

How:

Create your vision board.

Ground in breath

Breathe for control over your nervous system and to release stress.

How:

Take three deep grounding breaths every time you wash your hands.

Meditation

Meditate for a heightened state of awareness and focused attention.

How:

Meditate for ten minutes as a part of your daily bookend habits.

Helping others

Helping others to deepen your social interaction and connect with something larger than yourself.

How:

Volunteer to help others or assist with events and charities.

Mindfulness

Be present and mindful through taste, touch, smell, hearing and sight. Your five senses.

How:

Tap into your five senses for contagious joy.

Relationships

Discover the key to a meaningful life through meaningful connections.

How:

Build a network of positive influencers in your life.

Visualise success

Visualise your future goals coming to life and challenge yourself to grow.

How: Create your vision board

A vision board is a visual representation of your ultimate personal plan: how you want your life to look and feel now and in the future. It is a collage of images and words, representing your strengths, goals, values and the feelings you want to create, and serves as exciting inspiration or motivation to manifest, to make choices each day and develop habits to bring everything to life.

Most vision boards fall under the categories of a corkboard full of words and pictures, a dream wall, a digital board on your computer or phone, or a bullet journal. A popular part of the high-performance toolkit used by elite athletes, businesses, high-performing teams and celebrities, it is a powerful and creative habit you can adopt.

According to *Psychology Today*, mental practices like visualisation can increase motivation and confidence, and even motor performance. One study found that, in elite athletes, visualisation enhanced physical practice and took results to a new level.

Create your board by putting up your values, words that inspire, words you need to remember, quotes that mean something to you and pictures that excite you in every area of your life, both in achievement (cars, houses, holidays, relationships, health, fitness and hobbies) and fulfilment (happiness, gratitude, joy, connection, laughter, silence, peace, refuelling and recovery).

Once up, or on your screen, visualisation is your power habit.

Realise Your Dreams with the Habit of Visualisation

Step 1: Imagine your desires

Picture what you want. Pause and think about your dreams. Ask: What would I want and feel if nothing held me back?

Step 2: Paint a clear picture

Write down thoughts and make a vision board. Imagine your dream life. What does it look and feel like?

Step 3: Feel it like it's real

Picture sights, sounds and tastes. Experience the emotions. Feel it as if it's true. Ask: How would I feel if my dream life came true?

Step 4: Take small steps daily

Focus on now; take small actions. Ask: What's one thing I can do today for my dream life?

Step 5: Keep going, stay strong

Expect challenges, but imagine facing and beating them. Ask: What keeps me going when things are hard?

Step 6: Celebrate

Make celebration a habit.

Visualisation is your superpower for turning dreams into reality.

Ground in breath

Breathe for control over your nervous system and to release stress.

The breath you just took was a gift. It is your life force. It was the first thing you did when you entered this world and will be the last thing you will do when you leave. Breathe – the wisest one-word sentence there ever was.

The mind, body and breath are intimately connected and can influence each other. Your breathing is affected by your thoughts, and your thoughts and physiology can be affected by your breath. You have probably been told or told someone in the past few years who is stressed or overwhelmed to 'take a breath'. You may have not been aware of the high-performance instruction you gave them, but breathing exercises are effective in reducing stress and help us to gain perspective and tap into fulfilment.

Oxygen is the vital ingredient that energises your body. Breathing happens all day and all night without a conscious thought. Today you will take on average 25,000 breaths. When you focus on your breath, you are fine-tuning a high-performance stress regulator tool.

When you feel stressed, anxious or overwhelmed, the human brain does not have a reliable method of escaping this feedback loop without conscious intervention and the change of breathing patterns. There are many forms of breathing techniques to master, such as 4-4-4 box breathing, 4-7-8 breathing, pursed lip life breathing, diaphragmatic breathing or alternate nostril breathing. There are techniques to fire you up and get your energy moving, and techniques to calm you down.

Deep breathing can help suppress the fight-or-flight response (see page 262). Deep, diaphragmatic breaths fill the lungs with oxygenated air and calm the nervous system.

Inhale your future; exhale your past.

To take a breath is to pause. Just take a pause. Now master the pause.

How: Take three deep grounding breaths

Three deep breaths is all it takes. You can do this anywhere at any time. It is your secret – master it, own it, practise it and give yourself this precious gift.

Take three long deep breaths. As you continue to inhale and exhale, you may add a few words, such as these from Thich Nhat Hanh:

Breathing in I smile.
Breathing out I relax.
This is a wonderful moment.

I am breathing in quietly.
I am breathing out deeply.

I breathe in light.
I breathe out and let go.

The power habit of three deep grounding diaphragmatic breaths is high-performance self-management.

Become a master of three breaths

▲ When you wake in the morning, take three mindful deep breaths.

▲ When you turn on your computer, take three mindful deep breaths.

▲ When you address your team, take three mindful deep breaths.

▲ When you are at a red light, take three mindful deep breaths.

▲ When you get home from work, take three mindful deep breaths.

▲ When you go to sleep at night, take three mindful deep breaths.

Take action

▲ How can you use breathing to manage your emotions and stress for the longevity of your life?

▲ Where would you like to incorporate the habit of breath in your life?

Meditation

Meditate for a heightened state of awareness and focused attention.

Meditation is high performance for the mind. If you breathe you can meditate. Like we go to the gym regularly for a strong body, we can meditate regularly for a strong mind. The one routine common to billionaires, icons and world-class performers is daily meditation. Tim Ferriss, from the podcast *The Tim Ferriss Show*, interviewed more than 200 world-class performers ranging from super celebrities to athletes, special operatives and bio chemists.

Of all the routines and habits, most had some form of breathing (the base of meditation) or full meditation practice. They were committed to cultivating a present-state awareness that would help them be non-reactive in heightened stressful moments – the ability to observe thoughts instead of being tumbled by them, like stepping out of a washing machine and calmly looking inside.

With meditation, the goal is not to quieten the mind, but to observe your thoughts. It is part of the morning warm-up – sit still, gather yourself, prepare for the day.

Below are five tips to get you started:

1. **Start small:** Try a short simple meditation to start. You can use a guided app or a timer and take conscious breaths for one minute.
2. **Create the habit:** Meditate at the same time each day to establish a pattern and a habit for life.
3. **Habit-stack it:** For example, meditate for a minute when you first wake up, or after your workout, or when you get home from work (see page 246 for more on habit stacking).
4. **Return to your practice:** Your mind will wander; your thoughts will interrupt. Notice it and return to the breath, the mantra or the guided meditation. This is building the muscle of returning to focus and controlling the ruminating mind.
5. **Be aware:** Of how you feel before and how you feel after.

Meditation is used by leaders as a method for managing the stresses that come with their job so they can keep their performance at a high standard for the long term without suffering burnout. It is about fulfilment, stopping, observing, coming home to self and calming everything down. Meditation can also reawaken you to how blessed you really are.

How: Meditate for ten minutes as a part of your daily bookend habits

Including this mind training each day as a part of your habit plan – making it one of your non-negotiables – is a commitment to elevating, to finding depth and purpose, and to feeling fulfilled in life through breath and self-awareness.

We recommend the easiest way to get started is with a meditation app, such as Calm or Insight Timer. Try different ones and establish which suits you best.

Take action

▲ Consider how important brain training is to you so you can have perspective in life and feel fulfilment.

▲ Make a commitment to practise twice a day – to bookend your day (am and pm) with meditation.

Helping others

Helping others to deepen your social interaction and connect with something larger than yourself.

Individuals who volunteer not only feel more socially connected, warding off loneliness and depression, but also have been found to have lower blood pressure and a longer lifespan!

By volunteering, you are consistently socialising. It forces you to keep in regular contact with others and make meaningful connections. This social contact can have a profound effect on your overall psychological well-being. Not only does it improve brain function, but you will also develop a solid support system, protecting you against depression and anxiety.

Volunteering can give you peace of mind and help counter the effects of stress and anger. Working with pets and other animals has been shown to improve mood and reduce stress.

Volunteering is at the very core of being a human. No one has made it through life without someone else's help.

Top ten ways volunteering deepens self-fulfilment

1. Provides you with a sense of purpose.
2. Connects you to community.
3. Means you can support others, bringing fulfilment to both their lives and yours.
4. Improves your social skills.
5. Increases satisfaction, self-esteem and well-being.
6. Allows for personal growth.
7. Provides future job prospects.
8. Enables you to learn more about yourself and what makes you happy.
9. Provides an arena to make new friends.
10. Fosters gratitude and appreciation.

How: Volunteer to help others or assist with events and charities

Consider the following types of volunteering:

▲ Helping friends.
▲ Volunteering to work with animals.

▲ Volunteering for a community project, charity event or in hospitals.

▲ Sports volunteering.

▲ Green volunteering.

Take action

▲ Which of the ideas in the list above speak to you?

▲ What do you want to do this year to give back?

▲ What actions will you take?

Mindfulness

Be present and mindful through taste, touch, smell, hearing and sight. Your five senses.

Zen master Thich Nhat Hanh defined mindfulness as the energy of being aware and awake to the present. It is the continuous practice of touching life deeply in every moment. The practice also leads to heightened concentration, which in turn leads to clarity and insight. Everything you do, such as brushing your teeth, driving your car, cooking, exercising, showering, eating and drinking, when done mindfully with a relaxed and open mind, can bring you joy and happiness so your tank is ready and full to handle challenges and the curveballs that life may throw you.

Mindfulness trains our brain to develop laser-sharp focus and your senses are the gateway to the present moment. They are available to you at any moment, and they have the ability to transport you back into the present moment immediately.

If we train ourselves to become more aware of the ordinary, life can very quickly become extraordinary.

Fulfilment stays with you through the natural ups and downs of a human life. Mindfulness is the practice that allows you to live it wide awake.

Observing your thoughts, eating mindfully, walking mindfully, actively listening, observing your surroundings and focusing on your breath are all training the brain for high performance and to be present.

How: Tap into your five senses for contagious joy

The '5-4-3-2-1 method' is something easy to remember. Take three deep breaths and sit still:

Write five things you can see
e.g. *the sun, a picture on the wall, people walking past*

_____

_____

Write four things you can feel
e.g. *the wind blowing, the pencil in my hand, my feet on the floor, the scarf around my neck*

_____

_____

Write three things you can hear
e.g. *the noise of chatter from the café, the clock ticking, birds chirping*

_____

_____

Write two things you can smell

e.g. the detergent on my clothes, fresh cut grass, the smell of my tea

_____

_____

Write one thing you can taste

e.g. the mint toothpaste, the lingering taste of my tea

_____

_____

Relationships

Discover the key to a meaningful life through meaningful connections.

The secret to a rich life isn't excelling at work, building wealth or globetrotting. According to a 75-year Harvard study mentioned in Fast Company, living your best, most meaningful life boils down to one thing: relationships.

Satisfying connections not only bring joy, they're also linked to improved health and longevity. When relationships are positive, we experience happiness, tranquillity and satisfaction. Think about the special moments in life that feel extraordinary – chances are these moments involved other people. If you're seeking a fulfilling life, focusing solely on yourself is insufficient – remember to connect and cultivate relationships with others.

Relationships are pillars of happiness and complete living. They offer a wealth of benefits. Through relationships you gain companionship from friends and family, forming a circle of trusted individuals to support you through tough times.

How: Build a network of positive influencers in your life

Networking and a focus on relationship-building has the purpose of making new friends, industry acquaintances and even future business partners. Role models are there to inspire you and you yourself can be a role model to others.

Ten tips on building strong relationships and a great network

1. Have open and honest communications.
2. Respect and appreciate others.
3. Practise what you preach.
4. Accept support and be supportive.
5. Set and respect boundaries.
6. Be open to compromise.
7. Be kind rather than right.
8. Show your appreciation for others.
9. Let go of control.
10. Reflect and learn from your relationships.

It's the quality of your close relationships that matters, not the number of friends you have.

Take action

▲ Actively participate in networking events, both online and offline. Introduce yourself, engage in meaningful conversations and exchange contact information with like-minded individuals.

▲ Invest time and effort in cultivating genuine relationships. Be a good listener, show genuine interest and regularly reach out to friends and acquaintances to schedule catch-ups or virtual meet-ups.

▲ Seek out diversity and new perspectives. Engage in activities or join organisations that expose you to different viewpoints, cultures and experiences. Be open-minded and willing to learn from others.

To lead a life of fulfilment, honour your promises, connect with your own inner hero and share with others. Playing on your phone or watching TV during the best hours of your finest days will not help you build high-performance habits that elevate you and make you feel wide awake to what life has to offer you.

Get comfortable with your uniqueness, be wide open to loving and learning, and then get out there and share radiating infectious positivity.

Colleen: For many years, my A-type personality, achievement junkie mentality, workaholic behaviours and unwavering strive for perfectionism served me very well building my career . . . until they didn't. I was so focused and driven that I never stopped to smell the roses, find joy, celebrate or embrace fulfilment. After burnout, everything changed. I had to teach myself to embrace fulfilment in the small and grand things in my life, to be present and in the moment, instead of ticking off my to-do list and moving on to the next thing. At the end of each day I now ask myself what I have achieved and, more importantly, what I am grateful for. This ensures I am embracing fulfilment on a daily basis.

What ignites your passion and brings you a deep sense of purpose?

_____

_____

_____

_____

What unique strengths and talents do you possess that you can leverage for extraordinary achievement?

_____

_____

_____

_____

What meaningful impact do you aspire to make in your life and the lives of others?

_____

_____

_____

_____

How can you create a supportive environment that fosters your growth and success?

_____

_____

_____

_____

These questions can help guide you in uncovering your passions, strengths, aspirations and the necessary steps to cultivate fulfilment and high performance in your personal journey.

Fulfilment summary

1. Fulfilment is about connecting to purpose and meaning in life.
2. Know the difference between achievement and fulfilment when you define success.
3. Feel your life through visualisation, breathwork, meditation and mindfulness.
4. Helping others and building positive and strong relationships are the cornerstones of shared happiness and fulfilment.
5. Commit to experiencing life as a human being not just a human doing.

Create Your Personal High-Performance Plan: FULFILMENT

To elevate your fulfilment:

What do you need to STOP doing?

1. _____
_____
2. _____
_____
3. _____
_____

What do you need to START doing?

1. _____
_____
2. _____
_____
3. _____
_____

What do you need to KEEP doing?

1. _____
_____
2. _____
_____
3. _____
_____

Chapter 17

Invest in Self-Care

Self-care is not selfish.
You cannot serve from
an empty vessel

ELEANOR BROWNN

t's time to create some positive changes and feel even happier, more balanced, confident and successful than you already are – by investing in self-care! Real self-care requires practice, commitment and introspection. It entails putting yourself first and getting in touch with what you really need, not just what you really want. Self-care rituals, habits and routines are the building blocks to long-term energy, strong emotional resilience, productivity and high-performance health.

Self-care is not self-indulgent or selfish; it means taking care of yourself so that you can stay healthy, keep your tank full, build your career and be there for your family, friends and colleagues. Mastering the three non-negotiable foundations of eat, move and sleep will support you to live a life of longevity and fulfilment, and to reach your true potential. When you consciously invest in deep self-care and create solid foundations, you maintain a strong, confident and healthy relationship with yourself. This has a positive impact on not only the relationship you have with yourself, but a positive ripple effect with your relationships and connections with community and culture. Having these three pillars in flow will allow you to step into life's challenges with a positive mindset, graded confidence and great energy.

Making small, good choices is much easier than struggling to achieve difficult-to-reach ideals, like 'lose weight' or 'get healthy'. When you have small wins along the way your confidence and self-belief flourish and you are ready to be bolder and make some bigger changes.

Take some time now to reflect on your health, decisions, actions and behaviours. Think of this as a chance to reset, refuel and re-energise your life.

Small decisions about how you eat, move and sleep each day can have a huge impact on your quality of life.

Refuel: Eat

There is no one magic eating plan or formula as every person's body is different. Instead, it is about thinking of food as your fuel source and discovering what fuel works for your body. Once you have established this, it is about setting the structure to support this.

The preparation and organisation of eating well and having choices available to you can sometimes be the roadblock between eating well and eating compromised choices on the run. A healthy food plan has so many benefits – from having raised energy levels, increasing your productivity and reducing your risk of illness, to improved mood and better quality sleep. Quite simply, nutrition is essential for good health and longevity. It doesn't matter how much you exercise, if your diet is full of fast foods, takeaways, pre-packaged meals and processed snacks, or foods that don't suit your own body, you will struggle to truly nourish your body and give it the energy it needs to perform at its natural best.

We like to eat by the principles of S-L-O-W:

▲ Seasonal: Fruit and vegetables that are 'in season' are often the freshest, especially if they're locally sourced.
▲ Local: Shopping at local farmers' markets is not only fun, it is also supporting your community. Find a farmers' market by checking your local farmers' market association, or look for a nearby butcher or fruit and vegetable shop.
▲ Organic: Buying organically grown has so many benefits – it's bursting with nutrition, tastes great and is a source of sustainable sustenance. You are not only lessening pesticides in your body, but you're also improving your immune system. Think paddock to plate!

▲ **W**holefoods: Quite simply, this means eating food that has not been through many processes and has not had any of its natural features taken away or any artificial substances added in.

The benefits of eating S-L-O-W foods extend beyond your physical health. It will simplify your eating plan without clogging up your mind trying to follow diets, fads and ways of eating that just don't suit your body.

Almost as important as what you are eating is *how* you are eating. Are you eating on the run or regularly eating at your desk and not really thinking about your posture and the speed at which you are eating? If so, try taking undistracted time to eat mindfully, appreciating every mouthful. Avoid multitasking or using your laptop or TV while you eat. If you live with other people, consider having dinners together. They say that mindful people are less likely to be overweight as they take the time with each mouthful to chew and then digest. If you are eating mindlessly, you will probably eat quickly and then go back for more, not giving your body the time it needs to thoroughly digest the food and gain the optimum nourishment.

Ten tips for high-performance eating

1. **Prioritise protein:** Include lean sources of protein like poultry, tofu, eggs or Greek yoghurt in your meals. Protein helps with muscle repair and growth, and it keeps you feeling full for longer.

2. **Colourful plate:** Aim to have a variety of colourful fruits and vegetables on your plate. Different colours indicate different nutrients, so a colourful plate ensures a well-rounded nutrient intake.

3. **Mindful eating:** Practise mindful eating by savouring each bite. Put down your utensils between bites, chew slowly, and fully engage with the flavours and textures of your food.

4. **Power prep:** Prepare nutritious snacks and meals in advance so you have healthy options readily available when hunger strikes. This prevents impulsive and less healthy choices.

5. **Spice it up:** Experiment with herbs and spices to add flavour to your meals without relying on excessive salt. Spices like turmeric, cinnamon and cayenne pepper offer both taste and potential health benefits.

6. **Fibre focus:** Choose foods high in dietary fibre, such as whole grains, vegetables and legumes. Fibre aids digestion, supports gut health and helps control blood sugar levels.

7. **Plate proportions:** Fill half your plate with vegetables, one quarter with lean protein, and one quarter with whole grains or starchy vegetables for balanced eating.

8. **Quality over quantity:** Opt for nutrient-dense foods rather than calorie-dense ones. This means choosing foods rich in vitamins, minerals and other essential nutrients.

9. **Moderation is key:** Allow yourself occasional treats or indulgences but enjoy them in moderation. This helps prevent feelings of deprivation and promotes a sustainable approach to eating.

10. **Post-meal movement:** Engage in light physical activity, like a short walk, after meals. This can aid digestion and help control blood sugar levels by increasing insulin sensitivity.

Remember, everyone's needs are different. If you're uncertain about your diet, consider seeking advice from a healthcare professional or a nutrition expert so you can eat in a way that's right for you.

Re-energise: Move

Movement not only helps us to feel great, it also helps reduce the risk of certain diseases, supports weight management, promotes improved sleep, releases endorphins and relieves stress. It also allows us to take a break from everyday challenges and responsibilities and helps emotions move through the body.

Movement is about the way you feel in your body.

Take action

▲ Are you feeling as fit, strong, flexible and lean as you would like?

▲ How would you like to feel?

▲ What's holding you back from feeling this way?

We have a non-negotiable to move our bodies every morning with a walk or yoga. We find it is the best way to start our day and gives us clarity, and simply just makes us feel great. However, for some people finding the motivation to get moving can be difficult. There is no fail-safe motivational secret. It is about finding the movement recipe that is right for you.

Here are some thought-starters and tips on things that you can do:

▲ **Move with a friend:** Having a buddy to exercise with can help you stay focused and encourage you to continue.

▲ **Unplug:** Turn off the TV, computer and smartphone and swap this time out to move your body. Hit the gym, go for a walk or do some stretching or yoga.

▲ **Change sitting into moving:** Pair physical activity with activities where you usually sit. Consider doing easy exercises or stretches while watching TV. Also, set a reminder at work to stand up and walk for a few minutes every hour.

▲ **Enrol:** Explore the schedule at your nearby gym, community centre or yoga/dance studio. Classes provide structure and help keep you motivated.

▲ **Plan daily exercise:** Just like you schedule meetings into your diary, do the same for your exercise. Once you put it in your diary, you are committing to yourself and it will help you hold yourself accountable.

▲ **Mix it up:** Make sure you mix it up: yoga, Pilates, cardio classes, swimming, dance classes, stretching, outdoor activities, hiking, skiing, walking, running or even a team sport. Mixing it up challenges us, keeps things interesting and motivates us to try new things.

▲ **Be ready:** Get your exercise clothes out the night before so you are committed when you wake.

▲ **Make it fun:** It's hard to make exercise a daily habit if you see it as a chore, so make it fun. Put on some upbeat tunes to keep you motivated.

Recharge: Sleep

The benefits of sleep go far beyond boosting your energy and mood. Adequate sleep is essential to a healthy lifestyle, and can benefit your heart, mind and more. Sleep deprivation can cause a lack of motivation, weight gain, moodiness, lack of concentration, lower immunity, serious disease and an inability to cope with stress.

Sleep is no doubt a fundamental part of feeling healthy, confident and being able to cope in life. We need good-quality sleep to recharge and re-energise our bodies. Sleep is the essential, non-negotiable foundation that gives us clarity, energy and focus. Ideally you should aim to get to bed by 10 pm or 11 pm at the latest. This may mean you need to give yourself a curfew. The hours before midnight are worth double the hours after in terms of sleep quality and benefit. This is the time when your body is replenishing and working in its boardroom manner by fixing whatever is out of balance. Many people we work with set an alarm for bedtime – to remind them to shut down their technology or turn off their televisions and get into bed.

Winding down at the end of your day is also important and doing sleep-inducing activities to give yourself the best opportunity to sleep can be beneficial. It is ideal to have at least one hour of no technology before bed for the sleep hormone melatonin to kick in and help induce sleep.

Studies suggest that a healthy sleep cycle is essential to mental and emotional well-being. Adequate sleep not only improves your cognitive function, focus and decision-making abilities, but also boosts your mood and energy levels, allowing you to tackle tasks with renewed vigour and efficiency. Yet we constantly push ourselves to do more and sleep less. Treat your bedtime like an appointment with yourself and give it the same priority and importance that you give to your work-related appointments. It is, in effect, a meeting you have scheduled with yourself. It is one of the best tank toppers you can do, at no cost whatsoever!

Take action

Ask yourself:

▲ Am I getting enough sleep?
▲ If not, why not?

Here are some tips on ways you can improve your sleep:

Establish a routine

We're aware that routines help babies and kids fall asleep at specific times. This also applies to adults because it allows your body to naturally get used to sleeping and waking at certain hours. Develop a consistent routine for bedtime and waking up. Prioritise a regular bedtime, create a personalised relaxation routine, and set a consistent wake-up time.

Avoid technology

Electronic devices stimulate the brain and make falling asleep harder. Keep your computer, mobile phone and TV out of your bedroom. Avoid using them in the hour before bed. These devices emit blue light that affects melatonin production and delays sleep.

Create a peaceful space

Ensure your bed and pillows offer the right support and comfort. Keep your room at the optimal temperature of 16°C to 18°C. Pleasant scents such as lavender can help create a calming environment.

Don't watch the clock

Worrying about sleep can cause anxiety. Remember that being in bed with positive thoughts is better than restlessly checking the clock. If you can't stop looking, place it on the other side of your room. Remember that even if you are awake in bed your body is still resting.

Be mindful of what you eat

Foods to avoid: Practising good sleep hygiene involves making healthy nutrition choices, avoiding certain foods and beverages before bedtime. It is recommended to steer clear of spicy food, excessive sugar, alcohol, stimulants, hard-to-digest foods and large meals close to bedtime. Additionally, consuming caffeinated drinks, like coffee or cola, in the afternoon can impact sleep quality. It's also advisable to limit fluid intake before bed to prevent disruptions for bathroom breaks during the night.

Sleep-friendly foods: Healthy eating improves sleep, and some foods are particularly helpful. Foods like milk, cheese, turkey and pumpkin seeds contain tryptophan and serotonin, which are crucial for melatonin production.

Relax before bed

Taking time to unwind is important. Reading, a warm bath or calming music can help.

Release worries

Journal or make a to-do list before bed to clear your mind.

Embrace darkness

Sleeping in total darkness helps regulate melatonin and reduces the risk of depression. Use blackout blinds or an eye mask to block light.

Stay active

Exercise benefits sleep and overall health. Avoid intense exercise close to bedtime if it affects your sleep.

Focus on sleep quality

Sleep repairs the body and boosts brain function, mood and health. Adequate rest can help prevent weight gain, heart issues and illness. Sleep is about quality, not just quantity.

The essential pillars of self-care

Refuel

▲ Meal plan and prep.

▲ Eat foods that give you energy.

▲ Water is the best hydration.

▲ Snack smartly.

▲ Control portion size.

▲ Reduce salt and sugar intake.

▲ Eat fermented foods for gut health.

▲ Include healthy fats.

▲ Use supplements to boost energy.

▲ Break late-night eating habits.

Re-energise

▲ Move every day.

▲ Dance to your favourite music.

▲ Move your feet before you eat.

▲ Try yoga and tai chi for flexibility.

▲ Do weights and body work for strength.

▲ Pre-book your classes.

▲ Do five push-ups a day.

▲ Skip rope for one minute.

▲ Take a bike ride in nature.

▲ Set achievable goals and track your progress.

Recharge

▲ Aim for optimal sleep (seven to nine hours).

▲ Avoid alcohol or a large meal before bed.

▲ Avoid drinking liquids one to two hours before bed.

▲ Create a pre-sleep routine.

▲ Disconnect devices an hour before bed.

▲ Use lavender essential oils.

▲ Try 4-7-8 breathing before bed.

▲ Journal gratitude each night.

▲ Set a fixed wake-up time.

▲ No technology in the bedroom.

Eating affirmations

▲ 'I nourish my body with mindful choices.'

▲ 'I choose foods that fuel my vitality.'

▲ 'I savour each bite with gratitude.'

▲ 'I listen to my body's hunger and fullness cues.'

Moving affirmations

▲ 'I embrace movement for my well-being.'

▲ 'I find joy in staying active every day.'

▲ 'I honour my body's need for exercise.'

▲ 'I am becoming stronger with each step I take.'

Sleep affirmations

▲ 'I prioritise rest for a brighter tomorrow.'

▲ 'I create a peaceful sleep sanctuary.'

▲ 'I let go of the day's worries as I drift into slumber.'

▲ 'I wake up refreshed and ready to embrace the day.'

Shannah: The way you eat, move and sleep is all in your control. I decided to really focus on controlling the controllables to protect my energy, my mind and the way I feel each and every day to the best of my ability. Having been surrounded by high-performance athletes, I saw the dedication, discipline and choices they made and decided I too could have a high-performance body within the boundaries of chronic fatigue syndrome by taking full responsibility for myself in these areas.

I focused heavily on what food made me feel good and what food didn't, and each year it gets finely tuned with my 1 per cent changes at a time – over twenty years this has created a completely different way of eating for me.

My movement is also in my control. Running doesn't work for my body anymore unfortunately. It took two years to be OK with that mentally as nothing compares to a runner's high. I constantly adjust to what is best for me now and for my future self so I don't damage joints and muscles. I shifted slowly from high-intensity aerobic exercise (which leaves me exhausted) to yoga, weights, walking, Pilates and stretching. I still feel strong and it all just feels right for me. But the promise is to move daily in some shape or form.

Sleeping is the real magic for me. Having good sleep hygiene is crucial. Essential oils, journaling, no fluids after dinner, having my legs up the wall while watching TV, stretching and finally breathwork and body scanning as I close my eyes, all set me up for a good sleep. As much as possible I stick to the same bedtime and wake-up time, even on weekends, which has given my body routine and is how I get the best out of it.

Self-care summary

1. Self-care rituals, habits and routines are the building blocks to long-term energy, strong emotional resilience, productivity and high-performance health.
2. Mastering the foundations of eat, move and sleep will support you to live a life of longevity, fulfilment and high performance.
3. Sleep is the essential, non-negotiable foundation that gives us clarity, energy and focus.
4. Having the three pillars of eat, move and sleep in flow will allow you to step into life's challenges with a positive mindset and confidence.
5. If you want to move forward and make positive change in your life, you need to take action.

Create Your Personal High-Performance Plan: SELF-CARE

To elevate your self-care:

What do you need to STOP doing?

Eat:_____
_____

Move:_____
_____

Sleep:_____
_____

What do you need to START doing?

Eat:_____
_____

Move:_____
_____

Sleep:_____
_____

What do you need to KEEP doing?

Eat:_____
_____

Move:_____
_____

Sleep:_____
_____

Chapter 18

Celebrate

The more you praise
and celebrate your life,
the more there is
in life to celebrate

OPRAH WINFREY

Celebration is a powerful and important practice that human beings crave. It is a tiny habit that builds success and momentum. You can get so caught up in life – whether that's at home, at work or in your personal daily life – that you can forget to slow down and celebrate your achievements.

Four reasons you may not celebrate yourself

1. It doesn't fit your personality.
2. You don't remember to celebrate (too busy).
3. You prefer to move straight on to the next task.
4. You don't want any attention.

Four reasons you should celebrate yourself

1. It boosts your energy.
2. It builds your confidence.
3. It keeps you motivated to stay on track.
4. It allows the journey to your goal to be joyful.

High achievers understand that life is a journey with ups and downs. Special moments like birthdays and anniversaries are markers on this journey – times to pause and think about life. They are a testament to resilience, strength and hope, especially later in life when they stand for decades of experience. Allowing people to enjoy these milestones boosts their well-being. Celebrating is a way to say that someone matters and that their life and progress have value.

Celebrating as a group delivers to you a sense of belonging – something that is crucial to human fulfilment and longevity in life. From birthdays to funerals, there is no end to the celebrations of who you are, where you came from and what you've done, and even who or what you have lost.

Celebration also elevates habits. Celebrating a specific habit strengthens it. By fostering feelings of accomplishment and confidence through celebration, we make the ground better for planting habit seeds.

When you stop and celebrate your achievements it not only gives you an awesome rush of dopamine, it also builds your confidence, allows you to try new things and gives you the motivation to keep going. It provides you with the opportunity to reflect, correct course if necessary and decide what's next. Just as importantly, it allows you to enjoy the journey, which can be just as satisfying and rewarding as getting to the final destination.

Our challenge to you in this final chapter is to make celebrating a high-performance habit that features regularly throughout your day, week, year and life.

You and your life are worth celebrating.

Take action

Remember as a child what celebration felt like.

▲ What was celebrated in your life, family and community, and what joy did it give you?
▲ What were your emotions?
▲ What did sharing happiness and joy feel like to you?
▲ What are the words you would use to describe this?

How to Harness High-Performance Celebration

Small wins matter

Celebrate it all; celebrate a good hair day, a promotion, baking the perfect chocolate cake or ticking off your get-to-do list. Celebrate ending that toxic relationship, getting a new job or graduating, a sunny day, friends, the smell of coffee, your child's laughter or your cosy bed. Celebrate the birth of a child, speaking up in a meeting, getting a B on your English exam or committing to your morning walk. Celebrate that you did that push-up, that you cleaned up the kitchen straight after dinner, that you took a moment to smell the beautiful soap on your hands or that you paid a bill on time. Celebrate it all – no matter how big or small the milestone.

Until further notice, celebrate everything!

Celebrating the smaller wins builds and powers the 'smaller' muscles to take on bigger challenges. Big wins are only the tip of the iceberg – they are the mountain tops and the peak only stands because it is supported by large solid base layers that are much wider, bigger and stronger. Success is birthed by a succession of many small wins. If life is meant to be lived and love is meant to be shared, then small wins are meant to be celebrated.

Embrace your inner athlete

Watch a sporting event anywhere in the world and you'll see athletes celebrating. They inspire us and teach us how to embrace celebration. They display it in two ways: raising of the arms and the high-five.

Raise your arms: This is a sign of joy in any language and is universal across cultures. It is a display of human triumph, of pride. Body posture shows us the emotional and mental state of a person. Arms overhead symbolises joy, power, grit, pride and pure enthusiasm. A slumped posture, as we also witness often in sport, indicates loss, low energy and a lack of power and confidence. We see this in individual celebration too. When did you last raise your arms in triumph?

High-five: Imagine this: you just scored the winning shot in your basketball game. Your teammates run up to congratulate you. They yell 'Great shot!' and give you a big round of high-fives. You are thrilled, happy, connected and, most importantly, appreciated. In the workplace high-fives bring the team together as physical touch connects people more than anything else. It is simple, quick, doesn't cost money, is extremely easy and crosses age, race and social class boundaries. It works with families, friends, business teams and individual celebrations; for children, teens, adults and those ten, twenty or thirty years older than you. The high-five makes you smile and catapults your mood, brings instantaneous energy and is a team booster like nothing else. It is tactile and it works.

High-performing individuals have the habit of high-fiving themselves in the mirror, connecting with self, encouraging self, raising their energy and acknowledging themselves for showing up. When did you last high-five yourself or someone else?

Celebrate as a team

In the workplace, celebration is key for team work and connection as everyone strives to deliver outcomes and reach their goals. The most successful leaders celebrate victories, no matter the size.

Success is not an end but a process. It is a way of working that encourages reflection and satisfaction and that results in progress and continued motivation. Celebrating the first win on a plan, when someone made a difference, when work is truly exceptional, when the team has consistently committed to the unglamorous tasks running in the background and the goal is in sight is a high-performance living habit.

Six reasons to celebrate with your team

1. **To remember the overall goal:** Reminds the team they are getting closer to completion.
2. **To emphasise goal-setting:** Encourages the team to set fresh daily goals resulting in renewed motivation.
3. **To boost motivation:** Shows the team the efforts made are noticed and appreciated.
4. **To show your company's success:** An important part of staff retention.
5. **To break up the work:** Infuses productivity into what would be a normal day's work.
6. **To reward specifics:** Inspires healthy competition within the team.

The team will likely have introverts who will soak in small praise – a positive email or something more sentimental – and also extroverts, who like attention, announcements and big high-fives! See the following list for some team celebration thought-starters to inspire you:

▲   Arrange a meeting solely to say thank you.

▲   Celebrate with a handwritten note.

▲   Give a small gift.

▲   Give your colleague a shout-out.

▲   Offer a ticket to an event or workshop, or the chance to work on a special project.

▲   Let the team go home early.

▲   Go on retreat as a team.

▲   Display recognition on a praise wall.

▲   Give back to the community as a team.

A key way to retain employees is showing them appreciation. Equally, try making celebration a part of your culture or family unit at home.

Use the power of habits

As we explored in Chapter 12, the power of habits lies in their ability to shape our lives, create positive change and give us reasons to celebrate. By establishing and maintaining healthy habits, we can transform our routines and enhance our overall well-being. Habits provide structure and consistency, allowing us to automate certain behaviours and actions. When we celebrate our progress and milestones along the way, we reinforce the positive impact of our habits and further motivate ourselves to continue on the path of growth. Whether it's celebrating a week of consistent exercise, acknowledging moments of mindfulness throughout the day or rewarding ourselves for prioritising self-care, celebrating our habits reinforces their importance and encourages us to sustain them. With the power of habits and the joy of celebration, we have the potential to unlock personal growth, improve our mental and physical health, and create a life that reflects our aspirations and values.

Celebration thought-starters

▲ Start a celebration jar.

▲ Celebrate the nos – they mean you are closer to the yes.

▲ Schedule a fun night out.

▲ Do a victory dance.

▲ Open a bottle of champagne.

▲ Tell a friend and share the win.

▲ Write it in your wins journal.

▲ Take a gratitude pause.

▲ Take a recovery day.

▲ Surprise yourself with a gift.

Colleen: In this modern, fast-paced world we all live in, where we are constantly connected and comparing ourselves on social media, it's important to find the 'wins' in everyday life and celebrate them.

> Remember every day of your life is a special occasion.

When you are an achievement junkie like me, celebrating is not something you have time for – well, that's what I used to think anyway. I was so busy completing tasks, ticking off to-do lists and then moving on to the next task that I forgot to celebrate. In fact, I think as a society we have all lost the art of celebration to some degree. We tell ourselves how busy we all are and have become accustomed to a world of instant gratification that passes in a fleeting minute. It's so easy to forget to stop and take a moment to celebrate my wins, but when I acknowledge my successes, even if they're small, it is incredible the amount of satisfaction, pride and joy I feel.

It doesn't matter how big or small, I celebrate everything: cooking a delicious dinner, finishing a project ahead of schedule, receiving positive feedback or just taking my dog for a walk. Waking up every day is a celebration.

Celebration summary

1. Raise your arms and exchange high-fives!
2. Embrace the small wins.
3. Celebrating ourselves and others adds meaning to our achievements.
4. Celebrating builds stronger teams.
5. Celebrating fosters a positive mindset and boosts motivation to continue striving for success.

Create Your Personal High-Performance Plan: CELEBRATE

What small wins can you celebrate about yourself, your family and your career right now?

1. Self: _____
2. Family: _____
3. Career:_____

To elevate your celebration:

What do you need to STOP doing?

1. _____
   _____
2. _____
   _____
3. _____
   _____

What do you need to START doing?

1. _____
   _____
2. _____
   _____
3. _____
   _____

What do you need to KEEP doing?

1. _____
   _____
2. _____
   _____
3. _____
   _____

Your
Massive
Action
Plan

All you need is the plan, the roadmap, and the courage to press on to your destination

EARL NIGHTINGALE

Embarking on your journey towards personal transformation and achieving your desired outcomes requires a massive action plan. It's important to understand that this plan is not a one-time effort, but rather a commitment to ongoing dedication and continuous improvement. By staying focused, taking consistent action and embracing the process, you will uncover your full potential and reach the heights you aspire to.

To guide you on this path, here are eight key steps to integrate into your high-performance plan:

1. **Clarify your vision:** Define your personal vision by reflecting on your passions and aspirations.
2. **Set meaningful goals:** Break down your vision into actionable and relevant goals.
3. **Prioritise and focus:** Identify the most important goals and allocate your time and energy accordingly.
4. **Develop high-performance plans:** Create detailed plans with smaller steps and timelines.
5. **Cultivate positive habits:** Incorporate daily practices that support your goals and personal growth.
6. **Seek support and accountability:** Share your goals with trusted individuals who can provide support and keep you accountable.
7. **Monitor and evaluate progress:** Regularly review your progress, celebrate achievements and adjust as needed.
8. **Stay flexible and adapt:** Embrace challenges, adjust strategies and maintain a growth mindset.

Top Tips to Elevate Your High-Performance Life

Life

▲ **Identify and utilise your strengths:** Recognise and leverage your unique talents and abilities to maximise your potential and achieve success.

▲ **Live in alignment with your values:** Clarify your core values and make choices that align with them, ensuring a sense of purpose and fulfilment in your life.

▲ **Create a compelling future vision:** Envision and set clear goals for your desired future, providing direction and motivation for your actions and decisions.

▲ **Prioritise your health:** Take care of your physical, mental and emotional well-being through regular exercise, nutritious eating, adequate rest and stress management.

▲ **Cultivate a positive mindset:** Develop a growth mindset, embrace resilience and maintain a positive outlook, fostering optimism and overcoming challenges with a solution-oriented mindset.

▲ **Build confidence:** Recognise and celebrate your achievements, embrace self-compassion and engage in continuous learning and personal development to boost self-confidence and self-belief.

Leadership

▲ **Practise self-leadership:** Take ownership of your actions, behaviours and decisions, leading by example and continuously developing your leadership skills.

▲ **Develop a personal brand:** Define and communicate your unique value proposition, cultivating a strong personal brand that aligns with your values and goals.

▲ **Foster a positive culture:** Create an environment that encourages collaboration, innovation and growth, fostering a positive and inclusive culture within your team or organisation.

▲ **Exhibit positive behaviours:** Demonstrate integrity, empathy and effective communication, setting a positive tone and modelling the behaviours you expect from others.

▲ **Set clear goals:** Establish specific, measurable, achievable, relevant and time-bound (SMART) goals, providing direction and focus for your leadership journey.

▲ **Cultivate productive habits:** Develop daily routines and habits that support your leadership goals and enhance your effectiveness as a leader.

Longevity

▲ **Prevent burnout:** Prioritise a life in balance, set boundaries and engage in self-care practices to avoid burnout and maintain overall well-being.

▲ **Plan for the future:** Set long-term plans and goals, create a roadmap for your personal and professional development, and regularly review and adjust your plans as needed.

▲ **Seek happiness and fulfilment:** Pursue activities, relationships and experiences that bring you joy, purpose and fulfilment, fostering a sense of happiness in your life.

▲ **Prioritise self-care:** Take care of your physical, mental and emotional health through regular self-care practices such as exercise, relaxation techniques and self-reflection.

▲ **Celebrate achievements:** Acknowledge and celebrate milestones, accomplishments and personal growth along your journey, recognising and appreciating your progress and success.

These are the key areas to focus on within each of the three pillars, guiding you to lead a fulfilling life, excel in leadership and prioritise longevity and well-being.

By integrating the wisdom and insights shared within these pages, you have gained a deeper understanding of yourself, your leadership potential and the key elements for long-lasting fulfilment and success. As you navigate the exciting chapters of your own journey, may this book serve as a guide, empowering you to live a life aligned with your values, lead with purpose and impact, and embrace the practices that nurture your well-being and celebrate your accomplishments.

Here's to a life of thriving, leadership that inspires and a future of longevity and fulfilment.

LIFE – Your Massive Action Plan			
Topic	**Start**	**Stop**	**Keep**
Strengths			
Values			
Vision			
Mindset			
Health			
Confidence			

LEADERSHIP – Your Massive Action Plan			
Topic	Start	Stop	Keep
Leadership			
Brand			
Culture			
Kindness			
Goals			
Habits			

LONGEVITY – Your Massive Action Plan			
Topic	Start	Stop	Keep
Burnout			
Planning			
Happiness			
Fulfilment			
Self-care			
Celebration			

Visit humanelevation.com.au to download your free action plan templates.

Acknowledgements

To our treasured husbands, Michael and Nick: we are wholeheartedly grateful for your unwavering belief in our abilities, endless encouragement and immeasurable love and support throughout this extraordinary journey we share together. Thank you for being our pillars of strength and support, and embarking on this remarkable adventure by our side.

To our precious children, Jack, Mia, Jake, Trent and Macey: you are the source of endless inspiration and joy. Your individuality and unique perspectives have enriched our lives beyond measure. May this book serve as a reminder of the boundless possibilities that await you as you navigate your own paths and unlock the extraordinary potential within.

To our incredible clients, we extend our deepest gratitude. Your trust in our abilities and your support have fuelled our creativity and passion in helping you elevate your lives. It is through your stories, challenges and triumphs that we continue to grow as authors and guide others towards unlocking their extraordinary potential. We are honoured to have been a part of your journeys and are grateful for the opportunity to make a positive impact in your lives.

We would also like to express our appreciation to the exceptional publishing team at Penguin Random House. Your dedication, expertise and belief in our work have been invaluable in bringing our book to life. From the editors who polished our words to the designers who brought our vision to life, your tireless efforts have transformed this book into a reality, providing a valuable resource for readers to unlock their extraordinary potential.

And now, to you, our cherished readers, it is our sincere hope that within these pages, you will find inspiration, guidance and a renewed sense of possibility to take action, elevate your lives and unlock the extraordinary potential within you. Thank you for joining us on this transformative journey and embracing the power to create a future filled with limitless possibilities.

About the Authors

Shannah Kennedy is a master life coach and life planner with twenty years of experience, and has coached elite athletes, CEOs, entrepreneurs, high-performing executives and teams. Her expertise empowers clients to take control of their lives, achieve their visions, and reach their goals. She is the author of the global bestseller *The Life Plan: Simple Strategies for a Meaningful Life* and six other acclaimed Penguin Random House books.

Colleen Callander, with an impressive thirty-year retail career, served as CEO for two iconic Australian fashion brands: Sportsgirl and Sussan. Her wealth of knowledge and track record in building brands and establishing winning cultures has inspired and empowered people throughout her career. Colleen is also the author of *Leader By Design: Be Empowered to Lead With Confidence in Business and in Life*.

Both in their fifties, Colleen and Shannah are at the pinnacle of their careers, balancing family life and peak fitness while working with leaders at some of the nation's most prominent brands and organisations. They understand the significance of investing in an enduring life and action plan centred on the three fundamental pillars of success: LIFE, LEADERSHIP and LONGEVITY. They are a dynamic duo with decades of expertise, passion and commitment, and are transforming lives and leadership, elevating individuals and organisations to unprecedented levels of success.

Stay in Touch

Immersive programs

Masterclasses

Keynotes

Walk the world with us

FOR ALL ENQUIRIES

humanelevation.com.au

▲ **Your life** has purpose

▲ **Your story** is important

▲ **Your dreams** count

▲ **Your voice** is powerful

▲ **Your health** is your foundation

▲ **Your mindset** matters

▲ **Your brand** is unique

▲ **Your habits** create results

▲ **Your happiness** is contagious

▲ **Your spark** ignites others

▲ **Your life** is your creation

Discover a
new favourite